Time fo CHILDReN?

TOOLS FOR REACHING OUT TO UNDER-TWELVES

Toolbag Contents

Index

We are relieved when we watch a TV hospital programme and see doctors and nurses restoring very sick children to health. We feel good when we send money to a missionary or relief agency, especially if it will help needy children overseas. We admire those who give up time to rescue severely disadvantaged children from orphanages in Eastern Europe.

But what about the children who live around the corner from us?

Most of them have not heard the gospel story. They don't understand what they are saying when they use the words 'God' and 'Jesus'. Many simply don't know what a Christian is.

They do not need our money or our sympathy. They need to discover the fullness of life which God made possible through Jesus.

This book assumes that every church has the responsibility to introduce all children to Jesus. It accepts that this has not been happening as we would like it to. It faces up to the difficulties. It suggests ways to get started.

HOW THE 'TOOLBAG' WORKS

The *Toolbag* series is designed to help you (and other leaders in your church) to explore an issue that is vital to your children's and youth ministry. You will have the opportunity to

● **see what the Bible says on the issue**

● **explore the issue on your own or with others**

● **pray about it**

● **get some off-the-peg, practical ideas,** including how to help your church with the implications of having unchurched children in it

● **make your own notes** which will lead to action

● **hear real-life stories of churches** that are tackling the issue

● **be reminded of what you have learnt in the *Wow!* boxes.**

CHOOSING THE RIGHT 'TOOLS'

A toolbag has pockets which contain tools – that's obvious. It is probably a good idea to go through the 'pockets' in this 'toolbag' in the order they are numbered. You will want to come back to some of them; others may not be immediately relevant to the urgent task you have to tackle.

Have you ever had to undo a screw with a nail file or try to cut something with a blunt knife? The job could have been done much better if the right tool had been available!

The 'toolbag' suggests many 'tools' that have been used to prise children out of their neighbourhoods and plug them into the Christian community, but they may not all be the best 'tools' for you to use. Be selective. Consider what is possible. Decide what will be most effective. Keep in mind the workers who are available.

No toolbag does the work for you... at least we haven't found one yet that does! So here are the 'tools' – the rest is up to you, to others in your church, and to God.

NEED A HAND?

If you are planning major DIY at home, other members of the family will want to make suggestions. After all they will have to live with the result!

If at all possible, involve others as you take out the 'tools' from this 'bag'. Some of the 'tools' are designed to be handled by more than one person – they will be a bit unmanageable single-handed!

GETTING STARTED

Before you start any DIY job, you will need to make decisions according to the materials available. You will have to find out what kind of shelving your local supplier stocks. You will find indispensible the leaflet showing what shades of paint are 'in' this year. If your family is like ours, it will then be necessary to change your original ideas because the materials for what you had in mind are not available.

Pocket 1 will help you grasp the big picture of the job with which you will be involved.
Pocket 2 will send you out to explore your neighbourhood so that you come home with accurate information. You can then base your plans and decisions for action on your aims and on the facts, and not build up false hopes or waste time with ideas that just will not work.

DON'T GIVE UP BEFORE THE JOB IS FINISHED!

Are there any unfinished jobs around your house? For a long time everyone nagged you to do them, then conscience got the better of you, you found a bit of spare time and got started. But it turned out to be much more difficult than you thought. The source of advice was not available. You could not borrow the right tool. So it never got finished.

The need to reach unchurched children has been around for a long time. It is a task that must be done. But it cannot be dropped when things get hard. These children need to know that we care and that we will go on caring. God does not just want them taken off the streets – he wants them brought safely into his kingdom. Make sure you plan the job through to completion. This is where the satisfaction and the rewards will be. ■

So go on – dip into the 'toolbag'. The job *may* be easier than you thought!

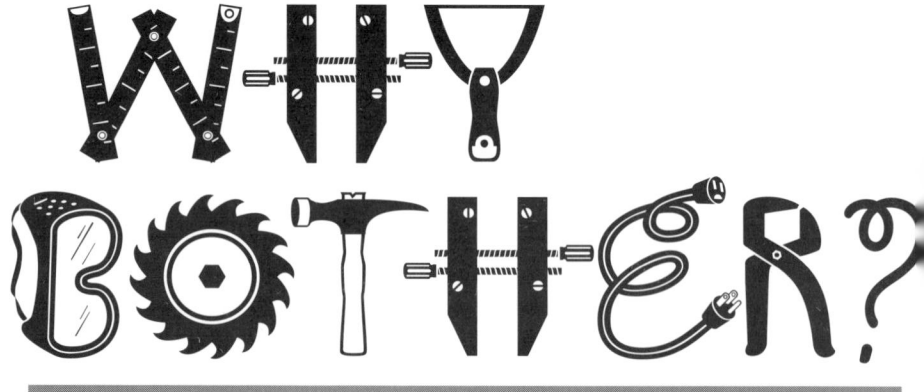

WHY BOTHER?

'Can any person touched by the Spirit of Christ be complacent about a situation which commits 85 per cent of all young human beings to set out on the journey of life with little or no awareness of a loving heavenly Father and no experience of the Christian story as told and lived out by the Christian community?'

(from *All God's Children?*, the 1991 report of the General Synod Board of Education and Mission of the Church of England).

I guess that, touched by the Spirit of Christ, you *do* care that all children should have the opportunity to hear and experience the Christian gospel. After all, that is probably why you picked up this book in the first place. You want them to set out on the life journey with God to heaven, through faith in Christ – a journey full of purpose, love and care.

PRESSURED LIFE

Children today are subjected to pressures unknown to those who were born before the 1960s. The media portray a much more exciting world than the real one. God's values are marginalized. Greed, materialism, immorality and sensationalism are made to seem the norm. Without careful parental supervision young children have access to pornographic and other horrific material through videos and the Internet. Occasionally young children are even responsible for taking the life of others.

Police and politicians cannot radically change the situation in the long term. Only Jesus can re-direct young lives for good, and only those who are touched by the Spirit of Christ can introduce children to him.

WHERE HAVE ALL THE CHILDREN GONE?

All God's Children? quoted research into child attendance at church. Churches of all denominations, it stated, are probably reaching no more than 15 per cent of children in their pre-teen years. What about the other 85 per cent? Jesus said, 'Let the little children come to me... ' (Matthew 19:14).

Back in the 1950s no more than 5 per cent of those who were involved with the Church as children became adult church members. It is unlikely that this situation has changed. Why are they put off? Jesus said, 'Let the little children come to me, and do not hinder them... '

In Matthew 18:6 Jesus had some very stern things to say about those who prevent a child's faith from growing to maturity. In *The International Bible Commentary* (published by Zondervan, and Marshall, Morgan & Scott), H L Ellison says 'there are those who have never come to faith because of the unfaithful conduct of the "faithful", and there are many spiritual cripples thanks to their early impressions of the church'.

All God's Children? concludes that the challenge to churches is to commit human, financial and prayer resources to the task of bringing the message of God's love to children who do not know him. Churches must also ensure that they offer not only a warm welcome to the children who respond, but also the very best kind of long-term help to grow within the Christian community. ■

TARGET PRACTICE

Read the following aims for reaching unchurched children. Then, by choosing or adapting one or more of them, write in pencil in the bull's-eye what *you* believe the main aim to be. Add other legitimate aims, in decreasing order of importance, in the outer circles.

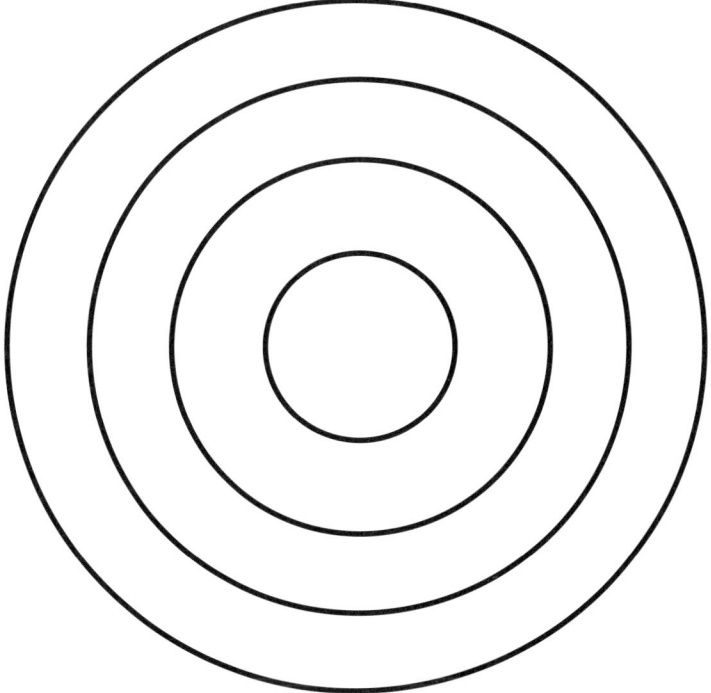

● As a church we want to feel better as a result of reaching more than 15 per cent of the children in our area.

● We want the Lord to enrich the life of our church by bringing more children into it.

● We want to befriend children so that they see Christians as friendly and approachable.

● We want them to get to know Jesus as well as building a positive relationship with those who serve him.

● Later in life we want them to be able to look back with warm affection at what the church meant to them as children.

● We want them to see that God loves them and has a purpose for their lives.

● We want them to become active members of the Church.

Now look up Colossians 1:28-29, 2 Peter 3:18 and Matthew 28:18-20. Does anything in these verses make you want to change what you have written in the bull's-eye? If so, rub it out and make the appropriate change, still in pencil.

LIFE TO THE FULL

We are talking about evangelism – strategies for helping children to hear and experience the Good News of Jesus. We want them to know that our heavenly Father loves us so much that he sent his Son to offer us 'life... to the full' (John 10:10). We want them to grasp that Jesus died on the cross to make it possible for them to be his children, so that they can begin to experience all that he has in store for those who belong to him.

Many children will have no understanding of even the basic facts of the Christian story, even less that it all started long before Jesus. But understanding, believing, responding and committing their lives to God *for the first time* is only part of his aim for their lives. The Bible verses we explored above encourage us to see the importance of making not just converts, but disciples – people who *carry on* learning to live God's way all their lives.

WITH OUR WHOLE LIVES

We shall communicate the Good News of Jesus to children not only through Bible stories but also by the quality of our own lives, as we demonstrate the effect of God's power at work in us. The combination of words of truth and actions of love will

● inspire children to find out more about God the Father

● draw them into a relationship with Jesus the Son, and

● enable them to experience the work of the Holy Spirit transforming them into his disciples.

All three aspects are aims of evangelism. Together they make the progression of faith which we long for more and more children to experience.

Now is there anything to change on your target? ■

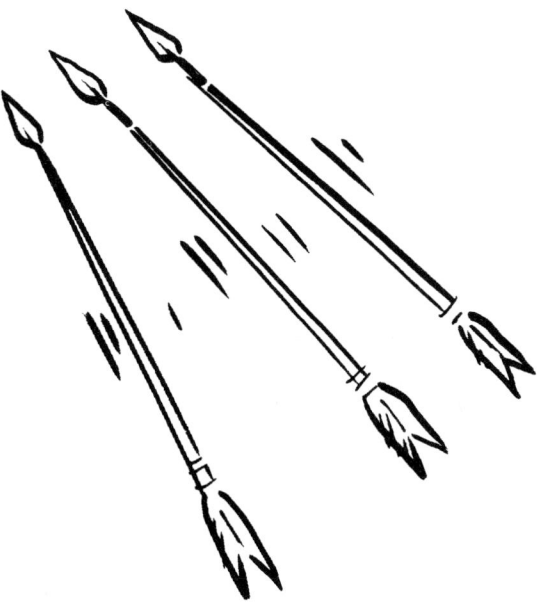

WHAT KIND OF GOD?

Exploring the Bible with care can blow our minds about the kind of God we want children to know.

● Turn to Psalm 145. In the space below jot down all the descriptions of God that the psalmist uses. You should find more than twenty!

● Now circle the truths about God that you think children who have little or no knowledge of him might struggle to grasp.

WHAT KIND OF CHILDREN?

We should not underestimate the ability of children to understand spiritual truth and to know God. Their small size and young age do not necessarily limit their understanding and experience of him.

If you have had the joy of talking with children about God, you will no doubt remember some amazing occasions when children have expressed very simply something that is incredibly profound. The Holy Spirit has clearly been their interpreter.

We do not have to wait for children to grow bigger before they are ready to be disciples. In Matthew 18:3 Jesus did not tell a child to become like an adult, but adults to become like children.

Children can understand and experience big truths about God even if they cannot read big words.

WHAT KIND OF EVANGELISM?

There are at least two sorts of evangelism that we should avoid:

The time-bomb method, sometimes known as the 'flip-top-head approach', assumes that children are basically mobile banks in which we deposit spiritual truth. If we cram enough into them early on, there will come a point in adulthood when all this amassed information will burst out and evidence itself in a vibrant faith and growing spiritual life.

The power-play method is characterized by highly intensive meetings where five year olds are asked to consider what would happen if the Seven Horses of the Apocalypse galloped through their bedroom that very night. After several hours of this encouraging approach, team members give children the offer of accepting Jesus there and then and of being good for the rest of their lives, or of being cast into outer darkness without a return ticket.

You may have spotted a slight exaggeration! Methods like these make some people question how appropriate any evangelism is with children. Alternatively they back off and present Jesus just as a friend who is as 'cuddly' as the teddy the children take to bed.

These two approaches demonstrate both a fundamental failure to understand children as being spiritually aware in their own right and also a feeble belief in what God is capable of doing in their lives. Far preferable is **a continuing relationship with children that encourages two-way conversation, allows the freedom to ask questions, and expects children to contribute real understanding and experience of God.**

God has a long-term commitment to children which means that he forces nothing on anyone. We should have too.■

DEVELOPING FAITH

Faith develops in a person. There are several theories about how this happens, some of which are more helpful than others. John Westerhoff observes four stages to a mature faith:

Experienced faith Young children observe and experience faith in those around. The way these 'others' treat children will either encourage or discourage faith in the children themselves.

Affiliative faith In later childhood children accept the beliefs of another person or group at home, at school or at church, and are carried along by their enthusiasm.

Searching faith People search for a faith which they can accept as their own. Westerhoff says that this does not happen until later in adolescence.

Owned faith People gain a personal faith that is expressed both in word and action.

In my experience, the different stages of faith are not tied rigidly to people's physical age. I have known quite young children who have searched for a faith of their own. After hearing a Bible story and seeing its truth lived out in other people, they have asked how they too can have faith. With sincere thought and prayer they have begun to experience a life-changing faith which is very much their own. Later, of course, they have taken steps of deeper commitment as they have matured and developed, but this first vital step has been the root from which their Christian life has grown.

Real evangelism with children presents the whole story of God the Father, Jesus the crucified, risen and glorified King, and the Holy Spirit. It shows Jesus to be right at the heart of the Christian faith. It also takes account of children's abilities and development, and gives them the opportunity to respond in their own way and at their own level.

God can, and will, work powerfully in children's lives.

BIG QUESTIONS

The kind of questions children ask will often show how their faith is developing. However, it is almost impossible to predict when they will ask these questions. Sometimes we may feel we have prepared the ground well, yet there seems to be little or no response from the children. At other times we shall be doing something very mundane when suddenly a very important question comes right out of the blue.

LIKE PAUL DANIELS?

I was once talking with a group of nine and ten year olds about Gideon. We had reached the point in the story where he was threshing wheat in a wine press, to keep it from the Midianites. At the mention of 'wine press' one of the children interrupted and said, 'My teacher at school says that Jesus didn't really change water into wine – it was just a trick like Paul Daniels does.'

Other children in the group were from the same class. They all seemed to be asking whether or not we have a miracle-working God.

When children have enquiring minds and let us catch a glimpse of what is going on inside them, there is a valuable opportunity to explain the answers the Bible provides and to help them understand what God can do for them. ■

SEEDS AND FRUIT

Children are successfully brought into church groups for under-fives, but churches often lose contact with them when they start school. Children come in large numbers to holiday clubs, but rarely become part of weekly church groups. Children hear about Jesus in mid-week and primary school Good News clubs, but the church loses contact with them when they move on to secondary schools.

We can begin school and club work haphazardly and say, 'We have sown the seed. God can take the seed and make it bear fruit in young lives.' This is certainly true. He can.

However, in the natural world, seeds that are sown in prepared soil and nurtured with care survive the longest and produce the best fruit. If we prepare carefully those who will hear God's word and plan how they will be nurtured, we are more likely to see them grow into worshipping, witnessing Christians.

In other words, if we reach out to unchurched children, we need to plan a strategy for continued contact.

NO REGRETS?

When I was twenty-one I joined a village church and discovered that they had been praying for someone to take over the morning Sunday School. As a newly qualified teacher in a neighbouring village they thought I might be an answer to that prayer.

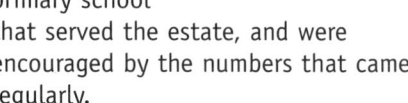

The youngest children were aged about four, so some of the eleven year olds were finding that the group had little to offer them. An elderly lady and a teenager helped lead it. When I took over as leader, I divided the group into 'Climbers' and 'Explorers' – my first ever attempt to get rid of the unhelpful name 'Sunday School'!

In order to keep the older children, I started a 'Pathfinder' group for the over-elevens. Since there was a shortage of leaders, Pathfinders took place on Sunday afternoons – a good time for reaching young people who had no other church connections.

Four years later, when Jill and I got married, those who had been eleven when we started were fifteen and rapidly growing out of the group. Our married life began with a Sunday evening group specially designed for them.

Before long Jill and I had to move away. As we had no long-term plan and had not trained anyone to take over, much of the work collapsed.
If only...

So beware of starting to build unless you have the tools to finish the job. You owe it to the children you reach.

CHILDREN BRING FAMILIES

A church in an expanding market town discovered that children who lived on a housing estate were at a loose end on a Sunday afternoon. They started to run children's activities in the primary school that served the estate, and were encouraged by the numbers that came regularly.

When a group of Christians from the parish church planted a church on the estate, those who had led the children's work were the first to volunteer to go. They were delighted and encouraged to find that several of the children who had come to the Sunday afternoon events brought their families to join the new church. After all, the children were in a familiar school building with Christians they had grown to know and trust. ■

GROUPS THAT CHANGE AND GROW

An inner-city church ran a lunchtime Good News club in the church primary school. Many of the children who came regularly did not attend church and were unlikely ever to do so.

When the children left to go to secondary schools, a mid-week Pathfinder group for over-elevens was set up. They came to it on their way home one evening a week. Some of the leaders of the school group were involved with the Pathfinder group as a natural link.

At first the group met back in their old primary school but later they helped to clear, paint up and furnish space in the church crypt so that they had a place of their own on church premises. Later, some of the young people went away on a residential camp and discovered what a personal relationship with Jesus could mean in their lives.

LONG-TERM PLANNING

Use this grid to help you plan your long-term strategy.

If you have a successful pram service...  | **What will happen when the children start school?**

What will happen when the children leave school?  | **If you start school work...**

If you have an after-school group...  | **What will happen when the children change schools?**

How wide an age group will it cater for, and what will happen next?  | **If you have a mid-week club...**

If you run a holiday club...  | **What will there be for the children in the weeks that follow?**

What will it lead to?  | **If you have a one-off event...**

TAKE IT AWAY!

Before going any further, share with your vicar or church leader all the big thoughts that have come to you as you have used the 'tools' in this 'pocket'. Show your target diagram. After further discussion, ink in your 'bull's-eye'.

Find a way of keeping your 'bull's-eye' aim in mind throughout the rest of your planning. ∎

POCKET 2 — THE CHALLENGE

SIZING UP THE JOB

It's time to roll up your sleeves and do something practical. Now that you have your aim in mind, you also need to size up the job in your area.

Check out the situation where you live and worship. Discover how effectively your church is bringing the Christian gospel to the children of your neighbourhood, and how you could be more influential.

YOUR CHURCH

UNDER-FIVES

☐ With how many children under the age of five do you have regular contact?

☐ How many leaders work with these children?

☐ What percentage of these are not children of church members?

☐ What percentage are present at a Sunday group or service?

☐ What percentage come to a weekday event?

How do the leaders feel about coping with more children?

_____

_____

FIVES TO SEVENS

☐ With how many children aged between five and seven do you have regular contact?

☐ How many leaders work with these children?

☐ What percentage of these are not children of church members?

☐ What percentage are present at a Sunday group or service?

☐ What percentage come to a weekday event?

How do the leaders feel about coping with more children?

_____

_____

EIGHTS TO TWELVES

☐ With how many children aged between eight and twelve do you have regular contact?

☐ How many leaders work with these children?

☐ What percentage of these are not children of church members?

☐ What percentage are present at a Sunday group or service?

☐ What percentage come to a weekday event?

How do the leaders feel about coping with more children?

_____

_____

(You could ask the same questions about teenagers, but this 'toolbag' concentrates on the younger ages.) ■

THE CHILDREN IN YOUR NEIGHBOURHOOD

This 'census' will help you to assess local opportunities, and to avoid making plans that will not work. It would be useful to have a large-scale map of your area on which to focus your investigations and to mark the information you collect.

Do not guess at the answers you do not know immediately. Make contact with those who have accurate information, like your local library and council offices. Take time to get it right. You will be basing your strategies on these facts.

SCHOOLS

● Mark on your map all the schools.

● Colour code those attended by children from the age group you plan to reach.

● List them in the boxes below.

● Add the type, fund-holder or source of control of each school in the next column.

● Then say what age group the school serves and what kind of contact your church has with it.

NAME OF SCHOOL	TYPE	AGE GROUP	CONTACT

SCHOOLS
Adapt these lists to meet the situation in your area.

TYPE

A Church or voluntary aided school (major church influence)

C Church or voluntary controlled school (minor church influence)

S County or borough school

GH Grant maintained

P Private school

AGE GROUP

N Nursery school or classes

I Infant school or classes

J Junior school or classes

P Primary school

M Middle school

SS Secondary school

COL College

CONTACT

CH Church children attend

CG Chairman of governors

G Member of governors

H Headteacher

T Teachers

O Other staff

PAR Parents

PTA Members of parent/teacher association

M Church already holds meetings there

OTHER CHILDREN'S MEETING PLACES

● **Mark on the map other places where children meet. You will need to add to the suggested list.**

ORGANIZED ACTIVITIES

R   Rainbows

BV   Beavers

CS   Cub Scouts

B   Brownies

SC   Scouts

G   Guides

D   Dancing class

GYM Gymnastics group

CYC Cycling proficiency

RID Riding

SW   Swimming

ATH Athletics

AFT After-school activities

_____

_____

_____

● Mark other churches on the map and indicate their involvement with children.

● Write in the day, time and place that children meet for these activities.

● Mark with an arrow the places where families gather locally, e.g. the park, cinema, shopping street or mall, recreation centre, swimming pool or library.

● Note how they travel to these facilities. Do they go by train, bus, car or on foot?

● Mark premises where you might be able to run sessions for unchurched children.

● Find out if these premises would be available and how much they would cost to hire.

● Enlist people who are in contact with non-church families in order to get an idea of their weekend programmes. Jot relevant facts in this box.

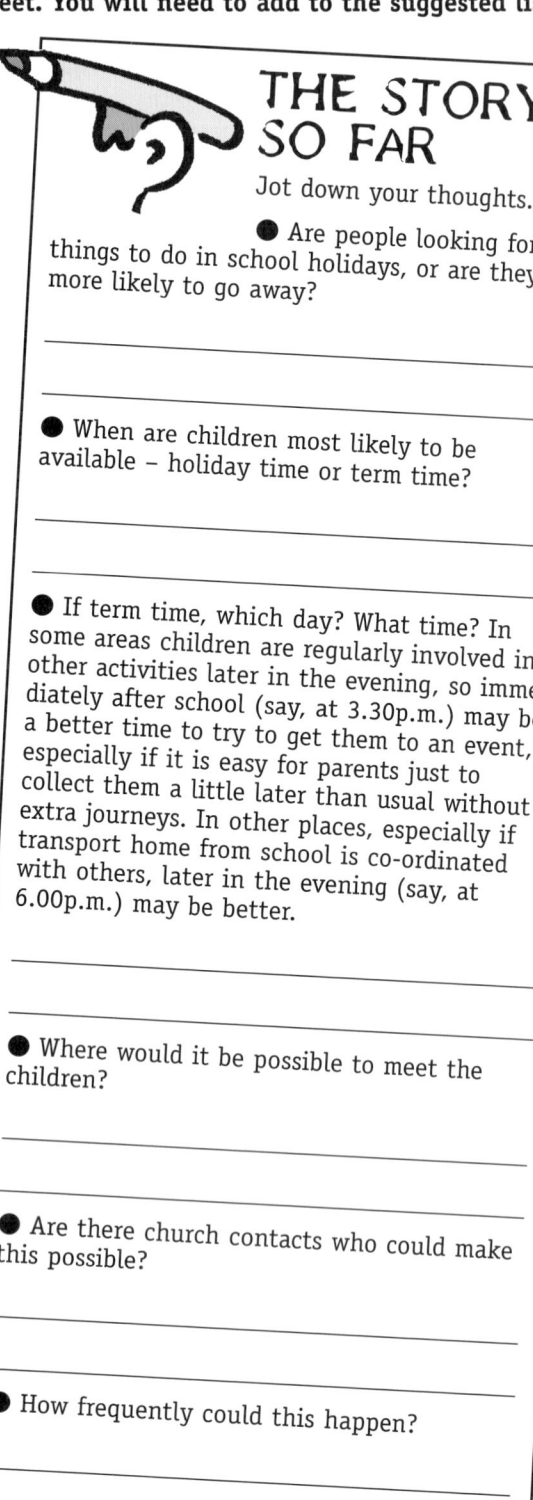

THE STORY SO FAR

Jot down your thoughts.

● Are people looking for things to do in school holidays, or are they more likely to go away?

_____

_____

● When are children most likely to be available – holiday time or term time?

_____

_____

● If term time, which day? What time? In some areas children are regularly involved in other activities later in the evening, so immediately after school (say, at 3.30p.m.) may be a better time to try to get them to an event, especially if it is easy for parents just to collect them a little later than usual without extra journeys. In other places, especially if transport home from school is co-ordinated with others, later in the evening (say, at 6.00p.m.) may be better.

_____

_____

● Where would it be possible to meet the children?

_____

_____

● Are there church contacts who could make this possible?

_____

_____

● How frequently could this happen?

_____

_____

_____

WHOLE FAMILIES, OR CHILDREN INDEPENDENTLY?

There is much to be said for trying to reach whole families with the Christian gospel. In recent years many churches have rightly emphasized the importance of united family life, and have formed their strategies accordingly. Some have not considered it appropriate to bring children into a relationship with God which would not be understood, supported or shared by their parents. This might make it hard for the child to grow in the faith, and might even set up tensions of allegiance within a family.

However, these churches have often not built strong enough bridges with whole families, so a generation or more of children has been deprived of the opportunity of hearing the Christian story and meeting up with those who live it out in their lives.

Reaching whole families is a brilliant ideal, but children should not miss out while we are finding the best ways of doing it. We need to be committed to reaching both whole families and also children independently.

By not reaching out to unchurched children, we may even be disappointing many non-Christian parents who hope that their children will gain from church activities something they themselves cannot give them.

WHOLE FAMILIES, OR CHILDREN INDEPENDENTLY?

Jot down your thoughts on reaching out both to whole families and also to children independently. What view does your church leadership team have?

RESPECTING PARENTS

'We should seek to evangelize children in a spirit of coming alongside their parents rather than that of coming against them. Several guidelines should help this happen:

1   *Only share with children what you can share with their parents.*

2   *Encourage children to tell their parents what they have done or learnt or care about.*

3   *Do not encourage a "defiant spirit" – a feeling of superiority in the child over his parents because he is, or is becoming, a Christian.*

4   *Keep a steady flow of information to parents.*

5   *Set up family opportunities – outings, parents' evenings, etc.*

6   *Always seek parental support and approval.*

To seek specific permissions is unrealistic but a golden rule of any evangelistic exercise, be it Sunday school, holiday club, beach mission or club night, is that parents must be informed so at least their permission can be presumed' (from All God's Children?).

WHEN CAN WE REACH CHILDREN?

On a Sunday, the priority for church people is to attend church. Worshipping with other believers is vital. Other events fit in around it.

However, the priorities of non-church families do not leave space for church. Sunday may centre around 'home' or 'leisure' activities either enjoyed as a family together or as individuals. Parents may be involved in jobs about the home – cooking, cleaning, DIY, gardening or car maintenance – and children may belong to sporting or hobby clubs and teams. It may be the only day when the family can all jump into the car or onto a bus or train and visit relatives or a beauty spot, a sporting event or a place of entertainment, or simply do the family shopping.

For divided families, Sunday may be the valuable time that children spend with the parent who does not have day-to-day custody.

For other people, Sunday has become a working day. Leaving their children in the care of the church for part of the day has sometimes helped solve the 'child-minding' problem.

The problem is that, as well as church activities just not being attractive, they may be impossible to fit into a family's established Sunday diary.

The 'convenient' times for children to attend an event arranged by the church are when their parents are at work or busy with other things, when it would be convenient for them to be 'out of the way', and when they are not at school (like during the holidays, on Saturdays or on mid-week evenings).

VERY STRANGE!

I once had to go to a law court as a jury member. If I have to do so again, I shall be as worried about it as I was the first time! The design of the building, the dress of the participants, the need to understand enough of an unfamiliar routine in order to be in the right place in the right posture at the right time without embarrassment, and the struggle to understand unfamiliar language and terms do not combine to make this an activity which I would voluntarily choose. My barrister friend may find this hard to understand!

WHERE SHOULD EVENTS BE HELD?

For those whose only experience of church is attending weddings and funerals, the idea of church probably gives them the same feeling of dread about entering such a building as I had about entering a law court.

We need to take into account not only *when* we might reach children, but *where* they will feel comfortable to be invited. ■

AGE GROUP?	WHERE?	WHEN?	WHAT FOR?

Jot down any more possibilities you may have thought of since 'The Story So Far' on page 12.

CORE GROUP

Collect all your information together – your map, 'The Story So Far' on page 12 and 'Age Group? Where? When? What For?' on page 14.

You may have to do this activity alone, but you will be in a much stronger position if you can meet with other concerned Christians to pray and discuss the situation.

The broader the knowledge within this group, the better. Try to include parents of children of various ages, local teachers, organization leaders, police and social workers, as well as clergy and church workers. This will take some arranging!

DOWN AT THE GYM

With the group above or on your own, explore Acts 19:1-10.

● From verse 8 discover where Paul had found it appropriate to share the gospel with the Jews who lived in Ephesus.

● How long did he persevere? How effective does this seem to have been?

● Where has it seemed appropriate to share the gospel with the children in your area? How long has this been happening? In the light of your investigations, how effective has it been? It was only weeks, not years, before Paul changed his strategy!

● Discover Paul's new strategy from verse 9. Paul and Tyrannus probably worked at their respective trades of tent-making and lecturing until mid-morning when it became too hot to work. Commentators suggest that the hall was like a lecture hall with a gymnasium where people spent leisure time. Paul used the vacated hall to spread the gospel to people who were in a familiar building at a time when they were not doing anything else.

● At what times are children in your area free? Is there a building which is familiar to them and available at these times? Could you use the school hall after school hours? Is there a community centre or village hall where they are used to meeting for Brownies or Cub Scouts? Is your church hall or church centre suitably positioned and welcoming? Which venue has the outside play space you need?

● From verse 10 discover how long Paul persevered and how effective he was. (He spent longer here than in any of the other places he visited.)

● Paul did not try to do this alone. Verse 9 suggests that he had a team of helpers, and verses 1 to 7 that they were young in the faith. Where might *you* find team members willing to help?

OUR PLACE

● Now display your map and enthuse everyone about your findings so far.

● Tell them the ideas you have noted on pages 12 and 14.

● Pray together for insight and wisdom.

● Ask the group: What else might be possible? Brainstorm imaginatively and freely before anyone launches in with the deadening 'It would never work because...'

● Try to agree on the best option. ■

THE NEXT STEP

Rummage through the rest of this 'toolbag' and decide exactly what kind of work seems to fit the research and thinking you have done so far. The 'tools' in Pockets 5, 6 and 7 will help.

Plans for reaching out to unchurched children cost time, energy and money. They will need the support and backing of the whole church if they are going to have lasting impact and if the team of leaders is going to survive.

At this stage a co-ordinator of the work should be appointed. It may be you, but it may not. Pray about who would be the best person for the job. Your vicar or church leader should make this appointment, with your guidance.

As soon as possible after being appointed, the co-ordinator should meet with a group of key people from your own church and look for their advice, agreement and support. This group will comprise the vicar or church leader, a member of the church council, a parent, and the leader of the regular children's work.

MEETING OF KEY PEOPLE

● From Colossians 1:28-29, remind yourselves of some of Paul's motives for his ministry.

● Discuss together the reasons for reaching out to unchurched children.

● Present your plans so far. Use your map, jottings and the thoughts of the core group from this 'pocket', and invite reaction to them.

● Ask and answer the following questions:

How does the planned work fit in with the church's strategy for children? Will it enhance the current week-by-week work or have different aims?

What follow-up and continuity of contact will be necessary and possible?

Will the current children's leaders be involved or will a completely separate team be required?

How will the team be recruited? (**Pocket 3** has some suggestions on this.)

Will the new plans have the full backing of the church?

● Now be realistic! Before you are finally committed to the plans, try to be objective about them. Check out these three questions:

Are you being realistic?

☐ Yes ☐ No

Always plan knowing your resources and your limits.

Are you being reasonable?

☐ Yes ☐ No

Consider the effect on the children who attend, their families, other people in the church, your leadership team and their families. Do not put people under immense pressure or place on them unreasonable expectations.

Are you being radical?

☐ Yes ☐ No

Constructive change and growth is a process rather than an event. Keep thinking, 'What is right for children now, in our community?' (Return to your research in this 'pocket'.)

● Ideally the church council will now pass a motion to endorse the work and to guarantee support and financial backing. Find out from your vicar or church leader when the church council next meets, and ask for the plans you have made together to be put on the agenda.

● Pray about the plans that are still in place at the end of this meeting and for the forthcoming church council meeting. ■

BIG PRAYING

Father God, you love all the children who live around here, even those from...
We confess that, until now, we haven't...
Reaching these children is a daunting task because...
Please inspire and equip your people to...
We will need great wisdom in making plans, especially...
We're depending on you to provide...

Thank you, Lord.

POCKET 3

WHO WILL HELP?

By now you will probably be saying, 'Yes, I can see what could be done, but who is going to do it? We're already short of leaders. Everyone in our church is just too busy!' Try to sort through this 'pocket' with one or two others who have caught your vision, perhaps your vicar or church leader.

FINDING LEADERS

Why *is* it so hard?

● Leading children is often seen as a job of secondary importance. Sadly, many churches first invite people to be church wardens, elders, treasurers, music or choir leaders, home-group leaders and so on. Then they see who is left to lead the children.

● Leading children is frequently considered to be women's work.

● Fear of the unknown sometimes scares potential leaders away.

● Some see established leaders trapped in their role for years, unable to escape. No wonder they hesitate to get trapped themselves!

● The thought of having to be an 'expert' or a 'teacher' is enough to put some people off.

ENVIRONMENT FOR GROWING LEADERS

Tick any of the following suggestions that you could put into practice (or ask to have put into practice) in your church, to encourage people to become leaders. Try the exercise individually first, then compare your answers.

☐ Pray for leaders, and get others in the church to pray.

☐ Ask if your church could appoint children's leaders first, and then see who is left for the other tasks.

☐ Perhaps men could be drawn in through some of the skills-sharing ideas from **Pocket 7**? With so many children growing up in single-parent families they desperately need male leadership.

☐ Invite potential leaders to observe some children's activities, then encourage them to put their toe in the water and see how warm it is!

☐ Suggest a limited 'probationary' period after which both the one who has appointed the leader and the one who is appointed have the opportunity of saying whether the job might be longer-term. If all goes well, encourage something like a three-year commitment. 'Less' is not 'good' in children's work where so much depends on building up good relationships.

☐ Try to explode the myth about needing to be 'experts'! The Bible talks about nurturing children in the faith in a family-like relationship, not a pupil/teacher one. Jesus definitely did not call 'experts' to be his disciples.

☐ In your week-by-week children's work, train people 'on the job' beside existing leaders. Then you will be able to pick out the right leader for a new project without leaving the regular group abandoned.

☐ Agree a minimum age for a leader, but after that consider all ages, sexes and shoe sizes! Pre-adolescent children relate very well to 'grandparent' figures as well as to younger ones – or I would have had to give up long ago! Retired people will often be free at the times when you need their help.

☐ Expect the rest of the church to support all leaders. There is nothing more disheartening and hurtful for a children's leader than to be given the job and then to be abandoned feeling vulnerable.

UNTAPPED SOURCES

So where would you say your top two untapped sources of leaders might be?

1 _____

2 _____

But wait a minute – you can't ask just *anyone*! ■

LEADER LOOKALIKE

Read through this list. A children's leader will

● be a committed Christian

● be a regular, worshipping member of the local church

● be of good character

● be able to make the time commitment – for planning, prayer and preparation as well as for helping to run the group – so it could mean handing over another church job to someone else

● be used to studying the Bible for themselves if you will expect him or her to teach it

● have the humility to be a learner as well as a teacher

● be full of care for other people, including children

● be able to work happily with existing leaders in the new team

● have a specific gift that is needed in the work

● be prayerful and patient.

Pretty daunting! We are not looking for leaders who are perfect in all these respects, but people who at least have the basic attitudes and priorities. Stop at this point to pray for insight.

● Decide together what four key words or phrases you would use to describe this kind of person.

1 _____

_____

2 _____

_____

3 _____

_____

4 _____

_____

● Individually, use these four words or phrases to stimulate your thinking. In your mind, look around your church's congregation. Note down the name of anyone who comes to mind as a potential leader. Share your suggestions. Do not dismiss any out of hand. After all, you have prayed for insight!

POTENTIAL LEADERS

1 _____

_____

2 _____

_____

3 _____

_____

APPROACHING INDIVIDUALS

● Do not ask publicly for volunteers. They may be totally unsuitable. Then what will you do?

● Ask specific people personally, starting with those on your list. This shows that the job is important and that you trust the person you are asking. They will realize that you think they can do it.

● Do not be put off asking people because you think they might say 'No'. They (not you) are the best judge of whether or not they should accept your invitation.

● Ask people even if you think they may have to give up doing something else in the church in order to become a children's leader.

● If people do volunteer, think carefully about whether they are right for the task. Do not be afraid to guide them into something more suitable instead.

WHAT WILL YOU SAY?

● Tell potential leaders why you are asking them and why you think they can do the job.

● Be clear about the role you have in mind. A simple 'job description' will help.

● If the group already exists, invite them along to see what goes on – without obligation.

● Let them know that you will chat and pray with them to help them think it all through.

● Do not put them under immediate pressure to make a decision. Give them time to think and pray.

● Explain that there will be an 'introductory period', to find out if leading *is* for them.

● Ask them to pray about it, talk to their family or friends and then get back to you.

● You will then need to ask them to fill in a 'Confidential Declaration' form like the one on page 20.

GUIDELINES FOR WORKING WITH CHILDREN

LEADER-TO-CHILD RATIOS

The Children Act 1989 recommends the following number of leaders to children according to age:

For 0 to 2 years – 1 leader to every 3 children (1:3)

For 2 to 3 years – 1 leader to every 4 children (1:4)

For 3 to 8 years – 1 leader to every 8 children (1:8)

For over 8s – 1 leader for the first 8 children followed by 1:12

LEADERS AND GROUPS

In addition to the ratios above, make sure that there is always more than one leader for a group of any size. If possible, have at least one male and one female leader with a mixed group.

POTENTIAL LEADERS

Potential leaders should offer the name of a person from whom a reference can be obtained. Questions to ask a referee might include:

● In what capacity have you known the applicant, and for how long?

● How willing is he or she to work with others?

● How suitable do you consider him or her to be for working with the specific age group?

● Are there any areas which might cause concern about the applicant doing this work?

CONFIDENTIAL DECLARATION

All employed people with access to children and young people have, by law, to make a signed declaration of any criminal record. A key recommendation in *Safe from Harm* (HMSO) also requires such a statement from volunteers. The policy issued by the House of Bishops in July 1995 states that all those in contact with children or young people in a church context must answer certain key questions. Failure to take the necessary steps could open Anglican Parochial Church Councils (or similar church bodies in other denominations) to a claim of negligence if a child comes to harm at the hand of anyone working with under-eighteens. You should put these questions on an application form for potential leaders in clubs or groups. You will find a suitable form on page 20.

When using such a form with helpers, emphasize that it is a positive action for good practice and that slur or suspicion is in no way implied.

The nature of the form is obviously sensitive and should be handled with care. Confidentiality should be maintained. In accordance with the *Data Protection Act*, no information should be divulged to third parties.

Do not simply hand out the form without explaining that you will need it back promptly. If possible, spend time working through the form with those who are required to complete it.

If any potential leaders give a 'Yes' answer, allow them to explain this disclosure personally, privately or by letter. If there is any doubt about the person's suitability for leadership, consult your archdeacon, your diocesan office (either the Board of Social Responsibility or Children's Officer), or appropriate officers in churches other than the Anglican Church.

We must always act with good practice in protecting children.

CONFIDENTIAL DECLARATION FOR CHILDREN'S LEADERS

CONFIDENTIAL

This form is to help you, the children's work organizers, and the parents of children attending to have every confidence in the care we shall provide. It is in no way a comment or judgement on your own qualities, but will be filled in by all leaders. If you have any questions about it, please direct them to

_____

Guidelines from the Home Office following *The Children Act 1989* advise all voluntary organizations, including churches, to take steps to ensure the safety of children in their care. In accordance with the House of Bishops' *Policy on Child Abuse*, you are therefore requested to make the following declaration:

Have you ever been convicted of a criminal offence (including any 'spent convictions' under the *Rehabilitation of Offenders Act 1974* or been cautioned by the police or bound over to keep the peace? (1)
☐ Yes ☐ No

If 'Yes', please state the nature and date(s) of the offence(s), continuing on a separate sheet of paper if necessary.

Have you ever been held liable by a court for a civil wrong or had an order made against you by a matrimonial or family court?
☐ Yes ☐ No

If 'Yes', please give details, continuing on a separate piece of paper if necessary.

Has your conduct ever caused or been likely to cause harm to a child or put a child at risk, or, to your knowledge, has it ever been alleged that your conduct has resulted in any of these things? (2)
☐ Yes ☐ No

If 'Yes', please give full details, including the date(s) and nature of the conduct, and whether you were dismissed, disciplined, moved to other work, resigned from any paid or voluntary work as a result. Please continue on a separate sheet of paper if necessary.

Signed _____ Date_____

Notes
(1) Because of the nature of the work for which you are applying, this post is exempt from the provision of Section 4(ii) of the *Rehabilitation of Offenders Act 1974*, by virtue of the *Rehabilitation of Offenders Act 1974 (Exemptions) Order 1975*. You are therefore not entitled to withhold information about convictions which for other purposes are 'spent' under the provisions of the Act and, in the event of appointment, any failure to disclose such convictions could result in the withdrawal of approval to work with children or young people in the church.
(2) a: A child for this purpose means anyone under the age of eighteen.
　b: 'Harm' includes ill-treatment of any kind (including sexual abuse) or impairment of physical or mental health or development.
　c: This question relates to any conduct, whether as a paid employee, a voluntary worker, or otherwise.

STAY LEGAL!

Although *The Children Act 1989* only legislates for under-eights, all work with children should be of the highest possible standard. This means paying careful attention to the following aspects of the work as you plan, and making sure that all leaders are constantly aware of the standards required.

REGISTRATION OF PREMISES

If you run an activity for more than two hours in any one day or a holiday club for six or more days in a year, you will need to register your premises with the Social Services. You can find their number in your local phone book. They simply keep a list of where and when activities run.

There is usually a small fee for registration, but the law assumes that registration will be granted unless there are good reasons why it should not be.

DESIRABLE STANDARDS

● **Space** You will need enough space for the number of children you have – approximately 2.3 square metres of unencumbered space for each child (i.e. with no stacks of chairs or furniture around).

● **Toilets** Ideally there will be one toilet and one hand basin for every ten children. Try to avoid the use of roller towels.

● **Play area** Outdoor play space is recommended when an activity runs for more than four hours. A quiet play area would also be valuable.

● **Warmth and cleanliness** Keep group areas warm, adequately lit and well ventilated. Maintain high standards of cleanliness.

● **Food preparation** If you are preparing food on site, the Environmental Health Officer will have to check the area before you can be registered. If children bring sandwiches, ideally these should be refrigerated. Drinks must be available at all times.

● **Special needs** Be willing and able to accommodate children with special needs. Check ease of access to your building and toilet facilities.

HEALTH AND SAFETY

● There must be access to a phone on the premises. This could be a mobile phone.

● Adults must be aware of safety and fire procedures. A fire drill should be carried out regularly. Fire extinguishers should be available and regularly checked.

● Children with infectious diseases must not attend.

● No smoking should be permitted near areas where children will be.

● Children should submit a health and parental consent form before an activity. Take health forms when going off site. You will find a sample form on page 22, which you can adapt as appropriate.

● Accidents should be recorded with a note of any action taken. The leader involved should sign the entry. A first aid kit should always be available and its location known to leaders. No medication should be administered without written parental consent. One leader should, ideally, be a qualified first aider.

LEADERS AND INDIVIDUAL CHILDREN

It is not advisable to talk to children alone in a secluded place. It might easily be misinterpreted. Sit with a child near the main group whilst other things are going on, so that you are in full view of other people. Children will not find this distracting.

ADMINISTRATION

● Keep an up-to-date record of children, their parents or guardians, contact phone numbers, attendance and other specific information (such as asthma, epilepsy, diabetes and allergies).

● Keep a daily register and make sure it is easily accessible in an emergency.

INSURANCE

All groups need liability insurance. Make sure your activity is adequately covered by your church's policy for both on- and off-site activities.

PARENTAL CONSENT FORM

Anything written on this form will be held in strictest confidence. The event leaders need to know these details, in order to be able to meet your child's specific needs, as far as possible.

You must bring this form with you the first time your child attends.

I give permission for my child to attend (name of event).

Child's full name _____

Address_____

_____ Postcode _____

Home phone number_____

Date of birth _____ Age _____

Name by which the child is normally known _____

Name of a friend attending (name of event) _____

Phone number where you can contact me in an emergency _____

Name and phone number of GP _____

Details of any known conditions, allergies etc. (e.g. asthma, diabetes, epilepsy) _____

_____

_____

Any other special needs or requirements that it would be helpful for the leaders to know about _____

_____

_____

In the unlikely event of illness or accident, I give my permission for medical treatment to be administered where considered necessary by the nominated first aider of the club, or by suitably qualified medical practitioners. Should my child require emergency hospital treatment, I authorize an adult leader to sign on my behalf any written form of consent required by the hospital if I cannot be contacted. However, I understand that every effort will be made to contact me as soon as possible.

I also confirm that the above details are correct to the best of my knowledge.

Signature _____ (Parent/Guardian)

Name printed in full_____

Date _____

POCKET 4

TEAM PLANNING 1

SESSION OUTLINE

When you have a team (however many people that is!),

1 help them to be enthusiastic about reaching out – use the Bible verses, the other relevant parts of **Pocket 1** and the 'Muddled Models' activity on this page

2 explain your thinking so far – use your map, jottings and the thoughts of the core group and key church members' group from **Pocket 2**, and invite reaction to them

3 finalize the details about the day, time, venue and nature of the activity you want to run

4 think through the legal requirements for both leaders and venue, from **Pocket 3** (pages 19 to 22)

5 arrange a time and place for Team Planning 2

6 pray together.

MUDDLED MODELS

Children will discover the Good News of Jesus not only formally by what we teach, but also informally by how we live as Christians. They will see what we are like when we have to do an unpleasant chore or are losing on the sports field, and they will hear what we say. Do our actions match our words? They will either know we are Christians by our love or get the idea that we are no different from everyone else.

Try this silly exercise.

● Take half a dozen children's coloured, wooden, building bricks and make them into an abstract model out of sight of your other leaders.

● Ask the others to imagine the model and draw it on a sheet of paper as you describe it to them. Your description might be something like this:

'The base is a blue rectangle. Above this, vertically, in the middle, is a red rectangle. To the right, parallel to the red rectangle, is a green cylinder. Surmounting these two pieces is a yellow triangle. On the base, to the left, is a green triangle. To the right of the green triangle is an upright yellow rectangle.'

They should be confused!

● Now hand them the written instructions or project them on an overhead projector acetate. Give everyone time to make changes to their drawing, at their own speed.

● Finally, show them the model itself and encourage them to correct their drawing for the last time.

● Discuss which part of the exercise they found easiest. Why was this?

If children just hear the gospel explained, they will probably be confused. If we help them to discover it in the Bible, that will be much more helpful. Ultimately, however, the gospel will come alive for them when they see it modelled by Christian people. Then they may decide that they want to experience it for themselves.

WOW!

When we are introducing children to Jesus, our lives shout just as loudly as our lips!

WHAT NOW?

Before going any further with your planning, double-check all the practical details. This will require a few phone calls and one or two visits. The 'Check It Out!' list on page 24 will help you.

Then go to the appropriate 'pocket' for the kind of work you are planning. Read, think and pray it all through for yourself, then prepare Team Planning 2 in **Pocket 8**.

CHECK IT OUT!

NEXT ACTION

CHECKED

Maximum number of children
- [ ] For safety in the venue OK
- [ ] For floor space OK
- [ ] For insurance OK
- [ ] For supervision by leaders OK
- [ ] For feeling part of things OK

Age range of children
- [ ] For the expertise available OK
- [ ] For the kind of activities we can offer OK
- [ ] For the number of leaders available OK

(see ratios on page 19)

Dates
- [ ] Children available OK
- [ ] Leaders available OK
- [ ] Avoidance of clashes with other church events OK
- [ ] Venue OK

Times
- [ ] Agreed with parents OK
- [ ] Agreed with school staff (if necessary) OK
- [ ] Agreed with leaders OK
- [ ] Agreed with venue OK

Costs
- [ ] Hire of venue and equipment OK
- [ ] Publicity OK
- [ ] Resources OK
- [ ] Refreshments OK
- [ ] Licences OK

Recruiting of children
- [ ] In school OK
- [ ] Through home visits OK
- [ ] By invitation OK
- [ ] By letters to parents OK

Legalities
- [ ] OK with *The Children Act* (pages 19 and 21)

Venue
- [ ] Catering OK
- [ ] Toilets OK
- [ ] Access for wheelchairs OK
- [ ] Blackout OK
- [ ] Power points OK
- [ ] Heating (if necessary) OK
- [ ] Play areas OK
- [ ] Unencumbered space OK

POCKET 5

HOLIDAY AND MID-WEEK CLUBS

So you want to run an event during the school holidays?

HOW ABOUT A HOLIDAY CLUB?

A holiday club is a tried-and-tested way of reaching unchurched children during school holidays. Unless they disappear off with their parents or get stuck into, say, a week-long sports club, children will be desperate for something to do that is not 'boring'.

Holiday clubs normally run for three, four or five days, during the half-term or longer breaks, and often end with a service in church or a family celebration.

WHAT YOU WILL NEED

● **Imagination** Start with a Bible base and some theme ideas, then jot down attractive ways in which the children might learn. Do not start with a theme and then try to find Bible teaching that fits!

● **A practical mind** Think how the wildest ideas might work out in practice depending on the space, the children, the help available and the costs, remembering that the learning should be one of the most memorable aspects of the event.

● **A positive way of thinking** Try not to be limited by what you or others have done in the past, but be enthusiastic to try new, big, exciting ways of turning great ideas into reality.

● **Nerve** Inevitably you will take a few risks – your church may never have seen anything quite like it before!

● **The ability to remember** You will need to keep in mind the type of children you expect, the abilities and limitations of your team, and the facilities at your disposal.

● **A buzz of excitement** Your planning group will need to 'buzz' as you begin to see what is possible, with God's help.

● **A theme** This could be a country or a place (Australia, Italy, the North Pole) or an activity (mountaineering, water sports, building), or be based on an object (food, fire, water) or simply a biblical theme or character (Jonah, heaven, miracles).

● **A name** The right name for your holiday club will reflect your theme. You will probably not come up with it as you sit thinking about it together as a team, but at the strangest moment. The name may well be wacky. It should arouse curiosity. You may need to go on using it for the follow-up club.

● **Resources** Either you will buy a ready-made holiday club package (see page 48) or someone in your team will have the ability and capacity to create material from scratch.

● **A plan for follow-up** Too many churches have run holiday clubs that were packed with unchurched children and very 'successful', only to find that, when the club ended, they never saw any of the children again. Children reached during a holiday club will need special provision if they are to stay in touch. ■

HOLIDAY CLUB IDEAS

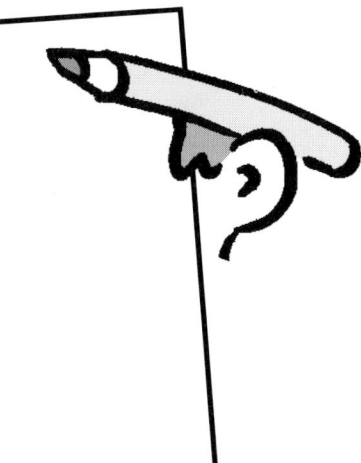

WHAT SORT OF CHILDREN?

Every aspect of each child is important. You are not only dealing with the 'spiritual side' of children, but also with their bodies, minds and emotions. So, in your planning, remember their need to be active, their emotional ups and down, their vulnerability, their lively minds, their curiosity, their love of surprises, their limited attention span, their particular learning ability and their physical needs.

All-together times are good for learning from up-front presentation, though you will always need to ask yourself if this is the best way for the children to learn and for the best communication to happen. Teaching could also take place in two larger, age-banded groups, or in small groups. Up-front, all-together presentation is also ideal for exciting children with drama, slapstick and big visuals, but they may also be frightened by loud noises, 'baddy' characters and sudden shocks.

All-together times might include general information, a club song, other songs, praying led from the front, or zany activities like a quiz, slapstick, sketches or a running joke. You could have a laughter box for children to post their jokes into which a presenter could read out – after censorship! There might be pantomime-style humour, with larger-than-life characters reinforcing the day's

teaching. An ongoing quiz will raise the roof, with a scoreboard linked to the theme and questions referring back to the teaching from previous days.

In **smaller-group times,** leaders have the opportunity to spend time with specific children, listening to their questions, hearing their perceptive comments about God, and helping them to see how the concepts that are taught might apply to them. Small groups are more practical for craft work, they make it easier to organize some games and to distribute equipment or refreshments, and they are good for encouraging group identity and a 'sense of belonging'.

In **active times** children can let off steam and be ready for quieter activities.

The best holiday clubs usually have a mix of all three types of activity.

SAMPLE PROGRAMME OUTLINES

Morning-only club

8.45	Leaders meet for preparation and prayer
9.30	Registration – children go to small groups for opening activity (craft, worksheet, quiz or other activity)
10.00	All-together time (welcome, songs, quiz)
10.15	Teaching time (short, visual presentation, activity or video)
10.30	Small groups (activity related to the teaching)
10.50	Active time (team game)
11.00	Drinks in small groups with the opportunity to complete the opening or later activity
11.15	Teaching time (up-front presentation)
11.30	Small groups (discussion about the teaching)
12.00	All-together time (drama, songs, jokes, quiz, prayer)
12.30	Home

All-day club

8.45	Leaders meet for preparation and prayer
9.30	Registration and choice of games
10.00	All-together time (welcome, songs)
10.10	Active time (team game, aerobics)
10.30	Teaching time
10.45	Small groups
11.15	Teaching time
11.30	Activity time (crafts)
11.50	All-together time (song, challenge)
12.00	Lunch and games
1.00	Teaching time
1.10	Small-group activity or outing
2.15	All-together time (summing-up, notices, songs)
2.30	Home

WHAT SORT OF GOSPEL?

When you have finished planning the content of your holiday club, ask yourself:

● If a child came with no knowledge at all of the Christian faith, what impression of God and Christians would he go away with?

_____

_____

_____

● Do all the activities help the children to learn the main point of each session? If not, what needs to change to make this happen?

_____

_____

HOW ABOUT A MID-WEEK CLUB?

Churches that make a huge effort with their holiday club will not want to lose touch with the children they reach through it. However, these children will not, cannot or, possibly, should not come to the regular Sunday children's groups. So how can churches continue to help them?

SIMPLE BUT COMMITTED WORK

A church in a run-down urban area held a summer holiday club. Since the church found it hard to recruit a team from among its own members, they drafted people in from outside to organize it. (This may sometimes be necessary, but the follow-up work is much harder when the children have not built up a relationship with the people they will continue to see on a regular basis.)

Week by week the church has kept in touch with the children who came in the summer. The programme for the club includes games (inside in the winter, outside in the summer), refreshments, an episode from a Christian video, and time to pray. The vicar and a few sporadic volunteers lead the twenty or so children, while one other person serves the squash and biscuits. It is hard work – especially with such needy children – and not ideal, but the children are still in contact with Christians and with the gospel.

It is exciting to hear children, many of whom come from homes where the names of God and Jesus are only swear words, praying for those in need and praising God for his answers.

TIME OF DAY CRUCIAL

In some areas it will be best for children to return home from school and then come to an event after they have changed and perhaps had some tea. In others, a club time a little later in the evening (but not too late for bedtime) will be most suitable. Elsewhere it works well to have an event immediately after school either on school premises, if these are available, or in other buildings very close to the school. This arrangement is the most successful in attracting children who have no previous connection with such an activity, especially if someone stationed on the school premises or at the school gate (with permission and authority!) reminds them.

Which you choose will depend on the times that children are most easily available and whether they live close to, or a long way from, the venue. Hold your event once a week, if possible, although this is a heavy commitment. It is hard for children and parents to remember which week the event happens if it only runs fortnightly or less frequently.

FINDING LEADERS

In an area where most people have a job, it is very hard to have a club at the best time for the children with the right number of leaders. Potential helpers will be at work.

If you count on having parents as leaders, think about their domestic arrangements. Someone somewhere will have to look after their children.

However, do not forget to consider as leaders those who are unemployed, students in their 'gap year' and people who do shift work and can be available at unusual times compared with those who work 9.00a.m. to 5.00p.m.

UNIQUE PROGRAMME

The programme for your weekday event may be unlike any other anywhere! It will depend on the flexibility of your premises, whether boisterous games are possible, whether you can be messy or not, whether there are other groups meeting in adjacent rooms who should not be disturbed, and so on.

It will also depend on your leaders' skills. The kind of games, sports, crafts, drama, music and methods of story-telling that you consider using must not be too ambitious for the people who are helping.

Whatever you plan, make sure you are not only going to be able to run it, but also control it. ('Maintaining Discipline' on page 42 will help.) ■

PROGRAMME TIMING

Each session will last as long as the children can handle. This may, of course, also depend on the time that the venue is available. Allow extra time for your own preparation, team planning and prayer before the children arrive, and for clearing up and debriefing afterwards. The length of the session may also depend on the amount of time to which the leaders can commit themselves.

It is better to plan a shorter time with the children and stop while it is all going well, it has not got out of hand, and they are still enjoying themselves. Leave them wanting more rather than sitting bored.

NUMBERS

You may need to restrict the numbers of children coming to your event. This may be for safety reasons, or to keep the child-to-leader ratio right (see page 19), or so that you can see how it goes without it getting out of hand. It is easier to increase the number than to reduce it when you have a hoard of excited children eager to keep on coming!

THEME

If you are following up a holiday club, you may want to choose the same theme. If not, invent a fun theme that may also suggest a name for the event. If you are going to meet every school week of the year, avoid a name that is too narrow and will gradually restrict the programme or the teaching. Something more general and fun is better.

PUBLICITY

If you start a mid-week event from scratch, you will need to think carefully about publicity. An item in the church notice sheet and one poster on the door, even with plenty of prayer, will probably not attract the children you are eager to reach.

Your research into church involvement in the local schools may come in handy here. You may be able to arrange for information sheets to be given to the children to take home from school. Staff at the school, or parents or governors who go into the school, could tell the children or their parents about it personally. You might even get an invitation to do an assembly (or part of one). Then the children will know your face before they come to your event.

In any publicity or promotional talk, be clear about the age group for which the event is intended. In well-populated areas, you may need to restrict numbers by narrowing the age range. In rural areas, however, you may have to consider a wider age range and make special travel arrangements to get the children home after the event.

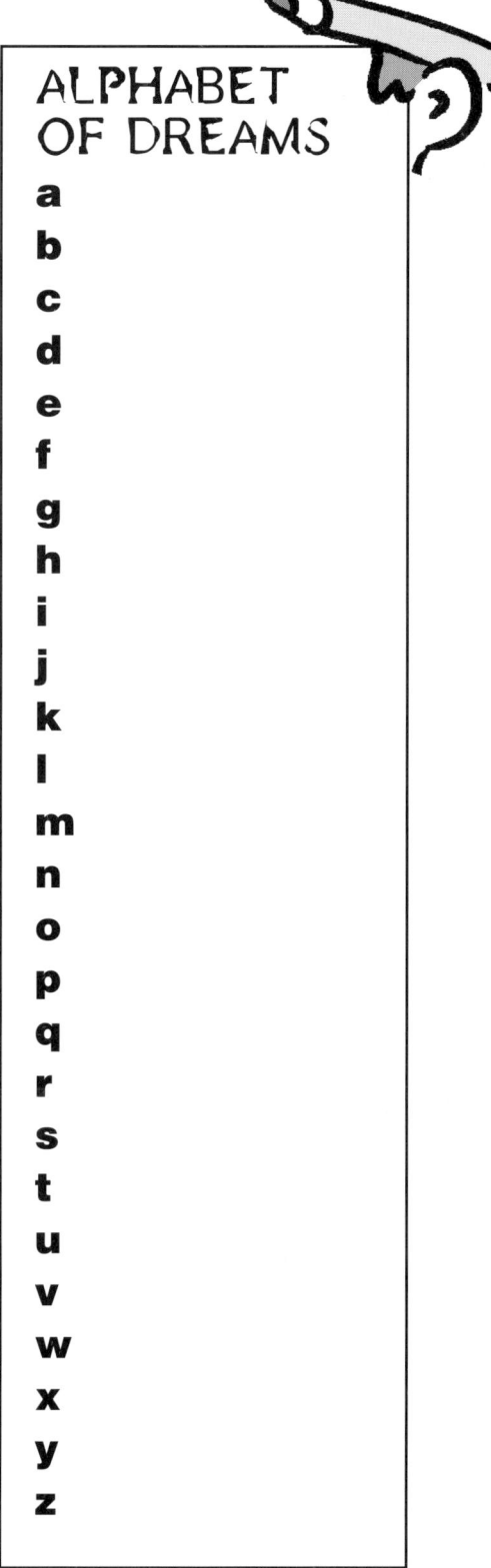

ALPHABET OF DREAMS

a
b
c
d
e
f
g
h
i
j
k
l
m
n
o
p
q
r
s
t
u
v
w
x
y
z

● Dream dreams. Find words or phrases that start with each letter and that would be ideal aspects of your mid-week event – your aims, the refreshments you would like, an activity you plan to include, colours of decorations, atmospheres... anything really, e.g. **a**we of God, **b**all games, **c**ola, **d**ares.

● Now find time to talk about your ideas with some children so that what you end up with will be right on their wavelength. ■

POCKET 6

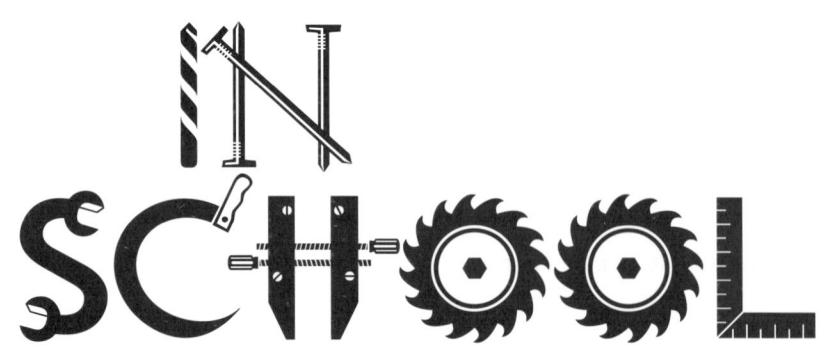

IN SCHOOL

'MISSION STATION UP THE ROAD'

As a primary school head-teacher I was invited to speak to a women's church meeting about life in a primary school. I began by saying, 'Last week you had a missionary speaker from Africa. Today I have come to you from the mission station up the road.' This was not quite what they had expected to hear, but I hope it made them think about the opportunities for the gospel that exist in local schools. Not that Christians in schools are allowed to evangelize, but they can present the Christian gospel clearly, build good relationships with children and live out the gospel in a school context.

ON THE MAP

● Look again at the schools you marked on your map when you were rummaging through **Pocket 2**.

● Write the names of the people from your church who have contact with these schools.

● Against each name, note down any opportunity for letting unchurched children hear and experience the gospel that he or she may provide.

YES, NO, OK BUT...

Clergy and church members can offer schools help not only with assemblies but also with classroom teaching and with running lunchtime or after-school clubs. Some schools will accept these offers of help whilst still being suspicious of the volunteers' intentions; others will simply turn them down.

But many will welcome the offers, so we must make sure that only people of tact with the ability to communicate naturally with children are involved in schools work. The headteacher and staff concerned should discuss the details openly with the person offering the help so that the visitor's enthusiasm does not overstep the boundaries which have to be drawn.

COLLECTIVE WORSHIP

'Collective worship should be distinguished from "corporate" worship. The term "collective" acknowledges that although staff and pupils have gathered together to participate in or observe an act of Christian worship, they do not necessarily share our Christian faith. In contrast, the worship of a committed body of Christians, in church for example, would be described as "corporate".

Beliefs and practices presented in school worship are supposed to be of a "broadly Christian character", in other words they are accepted across a broad spectrum of mainstream Christian denominations. It would not be acceptable to speak of practices unique to a particular denomination as though they were the practice of all Christians. ■

NAME	OPPORTUNITY

WHAT CAN WE DO?

It's important to realize that the school is not providing the church with an opportunity to evangelize, that is, to call young people to a personal commitment to Christ. Such a presentation will only alienate staff and pupils and, instead of building bridges, will put up barriers. There is no reason, however, why we should not clearly present the Christian gospel. The teacher in charge will expect a visitor from a local church to be open in their explanation of their beliefs and what it means to be a Christian.

We do, however, need to be sensitive in our presentation and because the majority of pupils are not likely to share our commitment to Christianity, we should not ask them to say or do things which assume their commitment. For example, "We know that God loves us" should be phrased "As a Christian, I believe that God loves us". This doesn't deny the essential truth of the statement, neither does it imply belief on the part of the pupils or staff. Try to avoid giving the impression that you are telling the pupils what to believe. Instead share from your own experience, using phrases like "I believe that..." or "Christians believe...". In this way we can still challenge the assumptions of our hearers and stimulate them to reflect on the Christian faith' (from *Support Your Local School*, Schools Ministry Network 1996).

Schools have to act within the legal requirements for 'collective worship' and enthusiastic church people must not run roughshod over them.

EFFECTIVE COLLECTIVE WORSHIP

● Have the attitude of a servant to the school rather than of a warrior trying to gain ground in the cosmic battle against evil!

● Let the headteacher know in advance what you are going to do and how you are going to do it.

● Confirm the day, time, length and venue of the assembly a few days ahead of your visit.

● Dress smartly.

● Arrive early.

● Treat everyone in school with care and respect.

● Do not belittle anything or anyone in the school for cheap laughs.

● Do not go over time – it will wreck the start of the school day and waste what you might otherwise have achieved.

● Make one clear point. Assume that you will be invited back, so you do not have to try to get across everything about God and the Bible in one ten-minute slot!

● Be visual or dramatic, but do not get the children so excited that you leave them on a chaotic 'high'. The teaching staff will not thank you for it!

● Expect the children to have little or no Bible knowledge. What is obvious and well-worn to you may be stunningly new to most of the children. Never underestimate God's ability to take age-old truth and make it impact on late-1990s children.

● Do not expect the children to be too clever at reading things off an overhead projector acetate. Help them in any way you can.

● Invite constructive criticism about your input from the teaching staff.

● Thank the school for inviting you.

● Ask the headteacher if it would be possible for you to come back again, and if so when.

PRAY FOR YOUR SCHOOLS

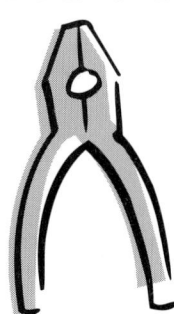

Whether or not you can do anything more in your local schools than is already happening, think of ways of being more specific in praying for these 'mission stations'. Prayers in church? The specific commitment of a home group? A monthly special occasion when those who are concerned for children, staff, volunteers and schools meet together to pray?

CLERGY LINKS

In the suburbs of a large town the clergy got together and offered their services to the local primary, secondary and special schools. They met informally with the head-teachers over lunch and discussed the possibilities. The head-teachers clearly preferred to relate to one member of clergy each rather than the whole group, so they agreed individual clergy/school links.

As a result, children now hear Christian teaching, meet clergy in a natural way and have their media image of clergy and churches dispelled. The clergy give groups of children guided visits round church buildings, and sometimes even help with pastoral care, in liaison with the school staff.

The lunchtime meetings between the clergy and headteachers continue at regular intervals so that they can contantly evaluate the scheme and build up their relationships.

SPECIALIST SCHOOLS STAFF

Throughout the country trusts have been set up to help make specialist Christian staff available to help with school assemblies, lessons and lunchtime or after-school club work. Concerned individuals or groups of churches pledge financial support for these staff over a number of years.

Once, a team visited a large number of schools weekly to take club sessions, but they only had the opportunity of leading assemblies twice a term. So the team began to question whether it would be more profitable to concentrate on a smaller number of schools and therefore on a smaller number of children.

In another town the trust workers were already doing exactly this, spending a whole day each week in one primary school doing an assembly, taking each class in turn and running a lunchtime club.

MUSIC AND DRAMA

In a multi-faith city area the staff members employed by a trust use their time with school classes to prepare and produce musical dramas which the children then perform for the rest of the school or for parents. Occasionally children from various schools come together to present a musical on a grander scale. The musicals have been carefully chosen for their Christian morals but also for their lack of offense to those of other religions. You can send for details of this kind of work to the Malachi Community Trust (address on page 48).

VOLUNTARY CLUBS

Many schools have Bible or 'Good News' clubs which run at lunchtimes or after school. Children can choose whether they want to go to them or not. Christian teachers on the staff or church people (or a combination of both) lead the clubs week by week. Sometimes children prepare a contribution for worship in the local church, and occasionally groups have gone away together for a weekend of fun and teaching. You can get help with setting up and running these clubs from the field staff of Scripture Union in Schools (address on page 48).

SCHOOL HELPERS

Instead of these 'up-front' ways of helping in schools, Christian parents may of course live out the gospel as they listen to children reading or as they help small groups with craft activities, swimming, cooking or games. Church people can also be employed as secretaries, lunchtime assistants and playground supervisors. Parents can help supervise children on outings and offer assistance with choirs, music groups, dramatic presentations and other regular or occasional school events. In this way the children in school can get to know and trust Christian people. ∎

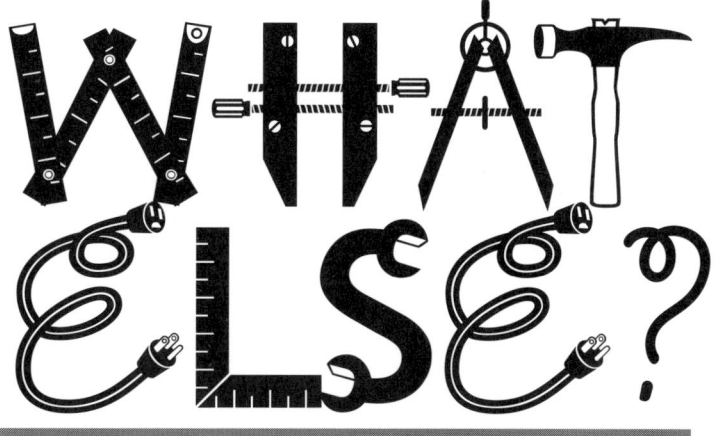

START THEM YOUNG!

Many parents are anxious for their new-born babies to benefit from what the Church has to offer, even if they do not see the relevance of Christianity to their own busy lives. Infant baptism or dedication can open the door for the Church to discuss matters of faith with them and to begin an ongoing link with their children.

The arrival of a baby changes a couple's life-style considerably, even more so that of a young mother who is on her own. New parents, suddenly unable to keep up the kind of social life they had before the birth of their baby, often look for companionship. Many are thrilled to meet other new parents to share baby talk and other concerns – a brilliant opportunity for Christians, especially those who are new parents themselves.

Churches have found various ways of meeting these needs, depending on the local situation, the available venues and the Christians who are ready to be involved. They are all extremely effective ways of reaching unchurched families and their children.

'CRADLE ROLL'

If a church member keeps a record of baptisms and dedications, this can be a way of making sure that the church keeps in touch with the families. Sometimes this has involved nothing more than sending birthday and Christmas cards, though many churches have done

So you want to do something more, or perhaps different from a holiday or mid-week club? The possibilities are endless... well, almost!

much more and have made the most of the opportunity. Christian parents who can identify with the new families could visit and invite them to special services, saying 'Come along with us to... '

PRAM SERVICES

No, not the regular maintenance of four-wheeled child transporters, but a mid-week  time for very young children and their carers to gather together for a half-hour mix of singing, praying, story-telling and activities, usually followed by refreshments and a time to chat.

In some churches the pram service has grown out of concern that the regular Sunday worship is not very suitable for young children. They are pushed out into the crèche and deprived of the experience of being with worshipping people. A pram service brings young children into the important environment of worship.

Sometimes pram services are held in the church itself – a non-threatening opportunity for unchurched parents to be there. Sometimes they take place in the church hall or centre, or in another suitable local-community venue, on a monthly, fortnightly or weekly basis. Familiar, friendly people lead them – possibly other mums from the pre-natal classes. As the service leaders explore the gospel with the children, parents hear it too.

A leader in a northern suburban church writes, 'Loneliness among young parents – particularly mothers and especially those new to the area – means that the pram service has been a huge success. It is a new venture for us, but women seem to think that church might be good for their children!' ∎

PARENT AND TODDLER GROUPS

The programme for parent and toddler groups will probably be less overtly Christian than that of a pram service. Perhaps once a week, children and their parents get together so that the adults can talk while the children play, sleep or are fed and changed. In her book *Under-Fives and Their Families* (CPAS 1990), Judith Wigley writes about the aims of such groups:

'Achieving our aim in parent and toddler groups is often a very long process. Many families entering our groups are a long way from God, with little knowledge or understanding of him or of Jesus as his Son. Gone are the days when we could presume that everyone had a basic knowledge of Christianity.

It was a great help to me in my early days of working with parents in toddler groups to understand some of the stages that people go through before coming to faith and commitment. These stages are often

● *awareness of the supernatural*

● *initial awareness of Christianity*

● *interest in Christianity*

● *awareness of basic facts of the gospel*

● *grasp of the implications of the gospel*

● *positive attitude to the gospel*

● *awareness of personal need*

● *challenge and decision to act*

● *repentance and faith*

● *commitment*

This enabled me to set myself short-term goals, identifying some of these stages on the way.'

Parent and toddler groups, however, must lead on to other things and not merely be a way of keeping contact with children until they start school and the links are broken.

PLAYGROUPS

When people in the local community think about setting up a playgroup, they often check out the possibility of using the church hall as a venue. It may be well used at weekends and in the evenings, but it stands empty during the day. Letting the hall for a playgroup certainly provides valuable income for church funds, but there may be other advantages and points of contact with unchurched families too.

Some churches have initiated church-based playgroups on their own premises. By staffing these with appropriately qualified church people, they provide much more than just playgroups. With parental knowledge and permission, playgroup teams can show the children Christian care, tell them Bible stories and teach them Christian choruses. Although parents are not always present while the groups are in session, playgroup teams meet them as they bring and collect their children, and have brief moments to show that the Church 'scratches where it itches'.

When arranging any event involving young children, it is vital to check the legal implications. Dip into **Pocket 3** of this book for some basic advice relating to *The Children Act 1989*. For more detailed help with playgroups including health, safety and team-work aspects, get hold of *Guidelines for Children in Crèches and Toddler Groups* by Ann Croft (CPAS 1995).

CPAS staff are also available to advise and train in this specific area of the church's work. Write to the Youth and Children Division at CPAS or phone (01926) 334242. ■

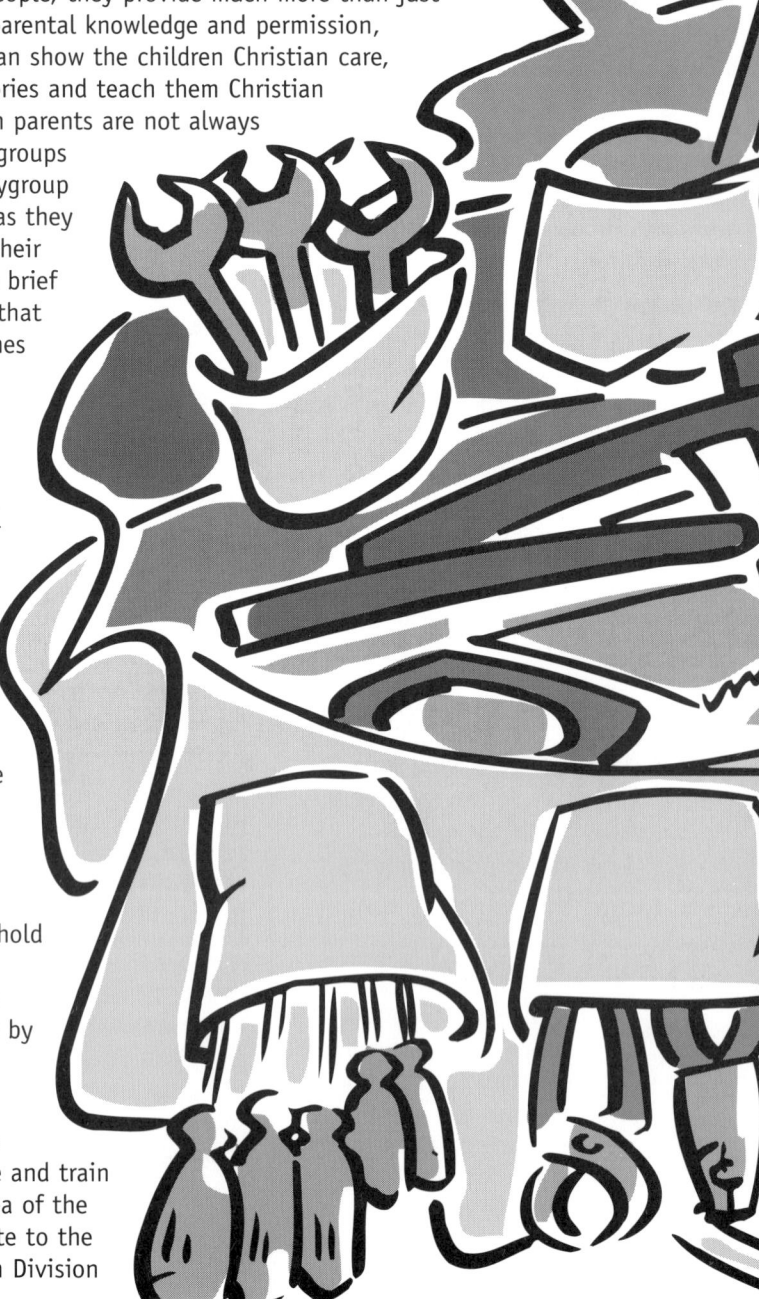

HELP WITH PARENTING

Most people become parents with little or no training for it. In a survey conducted outside our local supermarket, parents were asked if they would value the opportunity to attend a course in parenting. Their answers were overwhelmingly positive. After all, who wants to be a bad parent? But would they be less inclined to go if the course were provided by the church? In most cases the answers did not change. Consequently CPAS had the confidence to publish a video-based resource *Help! I'm a Parent* to train and encourage parents.

The resource's flexible design enables a variety of courses to be run – a weekly day or evening event, whole-day training courses, a regular parenting slot in parent and toddler sessions, or as the base programme for existing church groups. It includes resource sheets and course structures suited to different needs. It can be presented in either a seminar or discussion style – whichever is more appropriate for the group. The first takes a principle, teaches it and then asks parents to apply it to themselves; the second allows parents to describe their own situation and learn from the principles the leader introduces.

The use of videos and the design of the accompanying material mean that this resource works well for those who are not so happy with books or are not used to using them. It has been designed for 'fringers' and the unchurched as well as for church members. All the material stems from Christian principles and takes into account that it will be used by people of very different backgrounds.

PRACTICALLY AMAZING!

A suburban London church ran a parenting course in conjunction with its children's holiday club. One of the leaders said, 'We planned to make the course evangelistic, but it turned out to be much more practical. The core group included single parents, one of whom was a dad, and two Hindu women. We looked at the family, self-esteem, discipline, communication and faith. We could have spent days on some topics! We used clips from the video, some of the worksheets and added input of our own. A big plus was that people shared with each other. They found that other people had the same problems as them and could talk them through. People have asked for further parenting courses. I think we have touched on some important issues.'

Another church in a urban area ran parenting courses in the local primary school with the blessing of the governors and the headteacher.

An inner-city church in Merseyside runs parenting courses in parallel with its parent and toddler group. ■

MIND THE GAP!

Jot down

the facilities your church provides for parents with their young children

_____

_____

_____

the facilities which already exist in your area for them

_____

_____

_____

(So where are the gaps?)

possible ways for your church to contact young, unchurched children

_____

_____

_____

WHAT ELSE? WHERE ELSE?

Clubs and parent-supporting activities are not the only mid-week events that will help you reach children who cannot or will not come to anything on a Sunday. Look carefully at the children in your neighbourhood and at the life-style and gifts of church people who are not necessarily already working with children. You may catch a glimpse of opportunities which, with vision, prayer and preparation, could shake the world!

HOMEWORK CLUBS

A youth and children's leader on one of the biggest housing estates in the British Isles runs an after-school club for five to eleven year olds. But as well the club, something very interesting has developed that other churches too are beginning to take up.

Mike the leader says, 'The educational expectations and achievements are very low on the estate. With adult male unemployment at around 60 per cent, this is hardly surprising. The environment at home for many of the children to do homework is less than helpful, so we decided to add a homework club alongside the after-school club.

We provide a quiet, warm room, with suitable tables and chairs where the children can sit and work. Two or three adults supervise. They are not teachers and, although they will try to assist, they do not profess any particular skills. Local Authority funding has provided a computer and Children in Need and War on Want have funded software so that we can offer quite a range of material from encyclopaedias to dinosaurs and musical instruments as well as fun writing and drawing programs.

We regularly see about twelve children aged between nine and eleven in the homework centre which is open two days a week. I hope this project communicates to the children and to the community that we care for them and that we are concerned for their whole being and development.'

You do not need to live on an enormous housing estate for this service to be needed and appreciated. In the survey of your area have you become aware of less than satisfactory homework environments for children? Are there what were once called 'latch-key children' who return home each evening to an empty house? These situations exist in the smallest villages as well as in the biggest cities and provide a good opportunity for Christians to provide facilities like those described above.

SKILLS-SHARING CLUBS

Many sports and hobbies are enjoyed by both adults and children. For a start, there is football, cricket, tennis, athletics, gymnastics, skating, dancing, horse riding, cycling, fishing, modelling, mechanics, photography, video, model railways...

Some adults may be interested in amateur dramatics and could put on a pantomime with a group of children. Others may have musical skills and could form a choir or music group. They wouldn't have to major on Graham Kendrick!

Children would be very keen to make use of special facilities and to learn new skills from Christian adults who might eventually 'chat the gospel' as they all worked together. ■

WARNING!

Before setting up any activity that brings adults and children together, you must check out the legal implications outlines in **Pocket 3**. I know I have said it before, but it *is* absolutely vital!

PRETTY SKILLED PEOPLE

List in this box the names and hobby interests of five people in your church who you know well.

NAME	HOBBY/SKILL

Now pray for the people whose names you have written. Ask God about who you or your vicar or church leader could approach with the idea of sharing their particular interest with a group of unchurched children. In your mind's eye, can you see any of them winning the children's trust and friendship and eventually earning the opportunity to talk with them about their faith?

HIGH MOTIVATION

The great thing about arranging opportunities for skills sharing is that you are identifying people who are already highly enthusiastic and motivated about their hobby or interest, and committed to spending time (and money?) on it. Often they are keen to talk about it to people who are not in the slightest interested, but a skills-sharing club would give them the opportunity not only to talk about it, but to do so to a really keen audience!

NO CRINGE FACTOR

Christian children could invite their school friends to homework or skills-sharing clubs without embarrassment. They might find it hard to invite them to a Sunday group that would plunge their friends straight into an environment of Christian teaching and worship, but to invite them to do homework without a nagging parent lurking around or to learn a new skill from an enthusiastic Christian has no cringe factor!

Once children have got to know adult Christians in a natural way through sharing secular activities, they will not be far from experiencing and hearing about the love of God and about what Jesus has done for them. Mike shares this testimony: 'Although we have not as yet been able to develop fully the evangelistic edge to our project, about three months ago three ten year olds from the club approached me as I was going into our Sunday evening service.

"Can we come with you?"

"Well, it's one and a quarter hours and you'll have to behave."

"OK."

So in they came. They joined in with the fairly modern singing and sat through the adult sermon. The next week, with no further invitation from us, six appeared!

Now, ten to fourteen of them appear each week. Most call at our house first for a drink and a biscuit. The service continues as before but we do provide a worksheet and crayons during the sermon. They are all between nine and eleven years old and at least half are unchurched!'

God moves in mysterious ways! ■

PERHAPS NOT ALL WEEK OR EVERY WEEK!

This 'pocket' contains a lot of loose nuts and bolts for fixing people to dates and venues in order to provide imaginative events for unchurched children. The events themselves may not bring children to faith in Christ, but at least the children will see Christians as fun-loving, caring people.

If organizing and staffing a holiday club for a week or having the people and energy to run a regular mid-week activity seems too daunting to start with, do not give up hope! Perhaps one-off, shorter events would be better, especially if the alternative is to forget the 85 per cent completely. But you will still need people to help.

IT COULD BE... THEM!

Jot down

the names of people who might be willing to spend a little time helping to organize a one-off event

_____

_____

the time of year when this event could happen (From **Pocket 2,** you will need to check out the availability of those you want to reach.)

_____

_____

possible venues for the event

_____

_____

BRILLIANT ONE-OFFS

No detailed blueprint will fit your place and your people, so here are some sketchy ideas. Take the appropriate 'sketch', meet up with the people you have listed above and, after prayer, ask God to help you make the 'sketch' into a detailed 'scale drawing'!

A LIGHT PARTY

Many churches are becoming increasingly concerned about the dangers of the occult, and about  children wandering the streets frighten-ing older people with 'trick or treat' around Hallowe'en time. So teams of helpers have arranged alternative Hallowe'en events that focus on light rather than darkness.

A Light Party might just be a fun time to which unchurched children are invited. Or it might be a whole-family event at which 'fringe' families mix in a social, non-threatening environment with Christian people. It might involve

● games on the theme of light and brightness

● refreshments that avoid traditional Hallowe'en themes

● a brief focus on the God of light

● a lively version of 'Shine, Jesus, Shine!'

● an exciting way of learning a memory verse such as 1 John 1:5 – 'God is light, and there is no darkness at all in him'.

It is best to hold the event on 31 October, rather than the nearest Saturday. Otherwise it is not a real alternative. If it falls on a mid-week night, it could run from 6.00 to 8.00 p.m., with parents taking their children straight home to bed afterwards.

On the invitations encourage people to wear brightly coloured clothes. Because of the date, some parents and children may draw the wrong conclusions about the event. I once went to a Light Party where the Brownies turned up dressed as witches! ■

IT'S A WASHOUT!

Outdoors in the summer, 'It's a Washout!' might be just what your local children or families need to cool them down – as long as there is no hose-pipe ban! A fun event like this should not depend on specific skills that some children do not have. Games should be unusual with the extra element of 'danger' – getting wet!

● Organize several games, allowing extra time for people to meet, mill round and have refreshments in between them.

● Participants should wear swimming gear – you will need plenty of towels!

● Divide all the participants into teams. Not everyone in a team has to take part in every event, so nervous children can feel safe.

● Each game needs to have a clear numerical score which cannot be challenged! Perhaps for some games you could give a final score according to how wet the contestants are (0 = dry, 10 = soaking)!

● Not all teams have to take part in the same game at the same time. You could time teams individually at some games, or two teams could race against each other.

● For games that involve collecting water, measure the depth with a specially designed dipstick.

Here are some games ideas to get you started.

● Have a relay race that involves teams passing over their heads water-filled containers (tins or ice-cream cartons) with holes punched in the bottom. The winners will have collected most water at the end of their line.

● Get the teams to carry water in a plastic sheet (an opened-up bin bag will do) across an obstacle course to a collection bucket at the other end.

● If you can get hold of them, stack a couple of big tractor inner tubes on their sides. Have a garden sprinkler spraying water inside them. Participants have to climb in and retrieve objects from inside the tube tower.

● Have one team run a race or obstacle course while the other teams try to put them off by throwing cups of water over them. Beware of running across benches when there is water about!

SPORTS MARKET

If you want a simpler and less messy event than 'It's a Washout!', try a 'Sports Market'. This works better outdoors, but it might just be possible to run it indoors.

● Divide the children into teams of four or five.

● Organize the same number of games as there are teams, with at least one leader for each game and a couple of scorekeepers. You should spread the games around the field or hall with the scorekeepers in the centre.

● For each game, a team will score between ten and twenty points, according to how well they do.

● Each team starts at a different game when they hear an audible signal. A klaxon would be good. After an agreed time (usually three or four minutes), the klaxon sounds again, everyone stops playing and the teams all move round to the next game... and so on until everyone has played each game.

The nature of the games will of course depend on the amount of space you have, the equipment that is available, and the imagination of the organizers. Here are some ideas to get you started.

● Throw bean bags at tins on a bench or set up your own coconut shy.

● Pass a table tennis ball round the team without your hands. Players can only use the cardboard tube they have been given!

● Younger children will enjoy threading buttons on a string or joining bits of Lego together.

● Toss objects into different coloured hoops or buckets with different scores.

● Score as many netball goals as possible in the allotted time.

You could also include a short gospel message possibly using one of the games as an illustration. ■

IDEAS SUPER-MARKET

Take your pick!

● An ice-cream party in the summer with regular stops between activities for another scoop! Perhaps you could create an 'ice-cream factory' by providing a big selection of sauces, toppings and flavours for the children to make up their own king-size sundaes!

● A pancake making, tossing and racing event on Shrove Tuesday

● A summer event by a river or stream (but take good care!) involving a plastic duck race and a watery Bible story

● A barbecue and games evening at someone's home. If there is a swimming pool or at least a garden spray, so much the better!

● A hurriedly arranged snowman-building competition on a suitable winter's day

● A picnic for small children. If possible go somewhere with a bridge and a stream where you can play 'Pooh Sticks'. The children drop sticks into the stream above a bridge and watch to see whose stick appears at the other side of the bridge first – as in the A A Milne stories

● An alternative fashion event with prizes for costumes made on the spot out of waste materials

● A Christmas party at which all the small gifts for the children point to the real meaning of Christmas.

ENDLESS FUN

There really is no end to the kind of events that will be great fun for unchurched children and will allow them to meet Christian children and adults. As relationships develop, so the children will see more of Jesus, reflected in the life of Christians.

GROUPS WITHOUT FRONTIERS

Some events may be targeted specifically at unchurched children. Others may aim to create an environment into which church children will feel comfortable to bring their unchurched friends. You will find ideas to encourage existing children's groups to be evangelistic in *Groups without Frontiers* in this *Toolbag* series.

GET AWAY!

For many years I have used the same Christian camp site on the English coast. It was first established in the 1920s to provide a place for children from the city to have their only holiday of the year, in the country and in a Christian atmosphere. The aims also included to allow the children to live and play beside Christian adults, to teach them the Bible and to invite them to commit their lives to Christ.

When he gets to heaven, a friend of mine plans to say to the assembled throng, 'Hands up if you are here because you once went on a Christian camp or houseparty!' He reckons he will see a forest of hands go up, and I think he's right.

If you run some of the activities mentioned in **Pockets 5, 6** and **7**, you and your other leaders will start to build the good relationships with unchurched children which can only be improved by going away together. You might try for a weekend not too far from home, or be more adventurous and go further for longer. If your church-group members look forward with excitement to their annual camp or houseparty, why not encourage them to invite their unchurched friends along as well? They may be embarrassed to invite them to a church group, but a venture or camp is a different matter.

CYFA Pathfinder Ventures Ltd (address on page 48) run Falcon Camps which cater particularly for children who come from deprived situations.

Go on a venture with your children and you might make more hands go up in heaven! ■

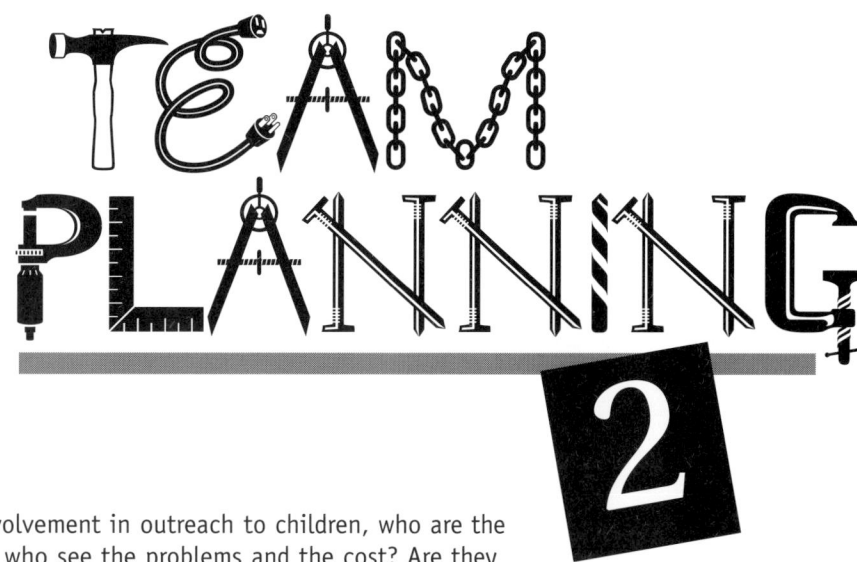

SESSION OUTLINE

Your next team time together might include

1 the Bible focus of Mark 6:30-44 'Where Would You Rather Be?'

2 training in 'Maintaining Discipline', from page 42

3 training in 'Explaining Christian Truth to Children', from page 43

4 a review of the support available to your leaders ('Help!' on this page)

5 practical preparation and prayer for your particular event.

WHERE WOULD YOU RATHER BE?

Explore together Mark 6:30-44.

● Find out what Jesus and the apostles would rather have been doing (30-32). How does this compare with what you would rather be doing than running an event for children every week? Be honest!

● In verse 33 do you recognize any of the needy children and families in your area? Do you have some of the compassion that Jesus had for those who were like 'sheep without a shepherd'?

● After reading verses 35 to 38, turn to John 6:5-9, a corresponding, but more personalized account. As you consider your involvement in outreach to children, who are the 'Philips' who see the problems and the cost? Are they right to do this?

● Who are the 'Andrews' who believe there must be a way forward, however unlikely it seems?

● It seems that everyone's attention was directed towards a child and to what Jesus was able to do. Both in discussion and in prayer, can you focus on a child or some children and try to discover what Jesus wants to do for him or her?

● In verse 14 John records the people's reaction. Talk together about what you want children to discover about Jesus, then with his help make plans for it to happen.

HELP!

Ask everyone on your team to be as honest as possible in completing this questionnaire.

HELP! Would you say you have –?	Yes	No	Not sure
encouragement and support in your Christian life			
good Bible teaching			
help with using the Bible for yourself			
a grasp of the aims of what we plan to do			
a clear idea of what is expected of you as a leader			
enough leaders to share the work with			
access to advice from a more experienced leader			
help from people with particular gifts			
a knowledge of what your own gifts are			
help in developing your abilities			
prayer support			
the assurance that the rest of the church knows and cares			
a shoulder to cry on and something to kick!			

As far as you and your team members feel able, share your observations. Are there any glaring omissions in the kind of support you are getting or will get from the rest of your church? If so, to whom can you turn for help? Strong leaders are always supported leaders. ■

MAINTAINING DISCIPLINE

● Get to know children individually. Good relationships are at the heart of loving, effective discipline.

● Familiarize yourself with their world, for example, through TV programmes, computer games, music and comics. You will always gain their attention by referring to things they enjoy.

● Make sure that the content of the session is suitable. If the material is inappropriate or irrelevant, they will look for other 'entertainment'. Any published material from books will need to be adapted.

● Do not bore them. Have something unpredictable in the programme. They are used to slick presentations on TV and in computer games. Yours will be competing with the professionals!

● Be confident. Any hesitancy may lead to insecurity amongst the children. If it seems that what you are doing does not convince *you*, they will not take it seriously.

● Beware of distractions. Anticipate them. Min-imize them. If all else fails, do not fight against them. Some distractions (like a collapsing visual aid or the use of a word with a double meaning) are avoidable; others (like a sudden snow fall or a fire engine going past outside) are not!

● As a rule of thumb, children will concentrate for about one minute for each year of their life. So the maximum attention span of a seven year old is seven minutes. Plan your programme in short bursts. Stop while something is going well – do not keep going until you have lost them!

● Avoid moments of idleness. See that the programme flows together and that all the necessary materials are to hand. You can never say, 'Sit quietly while I go downstairs to collect something.'

● Be prepared to change your plans. Respond to their curiosity. Do not carry on scratching the ear when the foot is itching. Be alert to what is motivating them *now*.

● Do not disguise an order as a question. 'Shall we now... ?' suggests there is an option not to do it! Instead say, 'Now we are going to... ', which leaves no option.

● Distinguish between children who are distracting (which is accidental) – for example, by doing up a shoelace in the middle of an explanation – and those who are disrupting (which is deliberate) – for example, by undoing someone else's shoelace.

● Similarly, judge between irresponsibility (the silly child) – for example, the one who interrupts with a thoughtless comment – and defiance (the wilful child) – for example, the one who deliberately does the opposite to what you have asked.

● Saying 'Yes' whenever possible makes it easier for the occasional 'No' to be accepted and obeyed. If you are always saying, 'Don't do that. Stop that. No, you can't go yet!', they will become immune to your negatives. When you have to say, 'Don't do that or you'll really hurt yourself', they will not hear.

● Combine firmness with understanding. Try to find out *why* children misbehave. They *may* just have brought a home problem with them. This means your reaction will need to be completely different.

● A pair of leaders with each small group (see the suggested ratios on page 19) gives moral support and makes it possible to separate difficult children. The leader who is less involved in running a particular activity can take a child to one side to deal with a difficult situation that has occurred.

● Present your message visually. Do not just rely on your voice. You will keep their attention better if they have things to look at.

● Involve children in activities. Busy, interested children are seldom disruptive.

● Let them talk on the subject. They will remember more easily things they have said.

● Let them *show* you. This provides an outlet for energy, and they will remember even better things they have acted out.

● Sometimes personalities clash. There may be some children with whom you will never 'hit it off'. Working as a team means someone else can step in when you can make no more progress yourself.

● Contact with home or school may enable you to understand a child's behaviour and to take united action to help him or her. Others, like social workers, may have been involved with a family over a period of time. Consult with them in extreme cases.

● Agree a chain of authority so that other leaders deal with the problem first and the overall leader only gets involved if the problem persists.

● Put an 'umbrella of prayer' over every child. When we are involved in evangelistic or missionary work, we are in the situation to which Paul refers in Ephesians 6:12. Ask for others to pray while the sessions are going on. ■

EXPLAINING CHRISTIAN TRUTH TO CHILDREN

● Try to keep the same adults working with small groups of children so that relationships can be built and trust and understanding can develop.

● Do not ignore issues because they are hard to explain or difficult to understand. Children look for honesty. Do not be afraid to say, 'I don't know'. Go away, find out the answer and have another conversation later on.

● Use the right language. Up to the age of about ten, children think literally and concretely. Use the picture of Jesus wanting them to become a member of his family – which they can understand, especially if they know of adopted children – rather than inviting them to ask Jesus into their heart – which might suggest major surgery!

● Do not do all the talking. Listen to the children. Ask them questions to draw out what they have understood and what they are thinking.

● Remember that it is not only in the 'teaching' times that children will learn. They will observe the Christian way in which you act, react and interact, and may ask the most revealing questions at the least convenient moment.

● Pray while you talk, as well as before and afterwards as well. We have an enemy who does not want children to respond to the Good News of Jesus.

● Pray naturally with children. Use short, simple sentences which they can copy rather than long, 'mature' prayers. Strike the right balance between talking with the holy King of Kings and with the friendly Jesus who wants us to share everything with him.

● A good structure for a prayer of response is 'Thank you', 'Sorry' and 'Please'. Use language which parallels the way you have presented the gospel. For example, 'Thank you, God, for loving me and for sending Jesus to die for me. Sorry, God, for my sins. Please forgive me, change me, turn me round, make me a member of your family, be my friend for ever, help me to do what is right.'

● Do not counsel an individual child out of sight of others. Your motives for being alone with a child may be misunderstood.

● After explaining the gospel to individual children, leave them a way of escape. I rarely encourage children to say a prayer of response straight away. I suggest they go away to think and pray about it and, if there is a written prayer, to decide whether they can really say each phrase and mean it. They may want to say the prayer alone (and tell me afterwards) or return so that I can pray it with them. If the Holy Spirit is really working in their lives, the opportunity will not be wasted.

● Make another appointment to give them assurance. Ask them: 'God doesn't say "Yes" to all our prayers, so how can you be sure he said "Yes" when you asked to be a member of his family?' Pray with them. Link the child into whatever opportunities for nurture you are able to offer.

The pack *God's Children* (see page 47) will help leaders to explain the gospel to individuals or small groups, to prepare them for a response and to nurture their new-found faith. Suitable for use with pre-literate and non-literate children as well as those with limited or normal reading abilities, the pack also contains guidelines for the leader and photocopiable sheets for the children to keep.

TOM AND MICHAEL

Sometimes we can overlook the work that God does in the lives of unchurched children when progress is in small steps rather than in giant leaps.

Tom did not want to go to camp on his own and there were no other boys of his age in church. So he took his school friend Michael. At camp they both responded to the gospel as the leaders taught it and lived it out. In the six months since camp, both boys have been coming along to a mid-week nurture group (Tom does other things on Sundays), and are growing in their faith.

Keep watching for the small steps. ■

POCKET 9

WELCOME TO OUR CHURCH

When children are baptized in the Anglican Church, the congregation says, 'We welcome you into the Lord's family. We are members together of the body of Christ; we are children of the same heavenly Father; we are inheritors together of the kingdom of God. We welcome you.'

We all mean these words when we say them, but the children's later experience of church may belie our good intentions. Do toddlers, who have not learnt to whisper and have a short attention span, really feel welcome? Would a previously unchurched ten year old from the holiday club feel 'at home' with the family?

WELCOME?

● Give each person a piece of card and ask them to write on it the name of a real or imaginary unchurched child. They should then add the child's age, background, special interests, character and learning ability.

● Collect the cards and re-distribute them around the group so that no one has the card they wrote.

● Now hand out or display the order of service for the act of worship to which such children might eventually come, if your outreach is successful. Remind the group what it will be like for these children to enter the building and find a seat – and just think who they will be sitting among!

● Now ask each person to adopt the identity of the child described on the card they are holding and brainstorm their likely reactions to church. Write up the comments (on an overhead projector acetate or large sheet of paper) without making or allowing any comments.

● Next, try to draw up a list of the group's concerns.

● Decide

if the experience of church would be beneficial to the children

☐ Yes ☐ No ☐ Maybe

if it would be right and possible to make changes to accommodate them

☐ Yes ☐ No ☐ Maybe

if an alternative service at a different place or time would be better

☐ Yes ☐ No ☐ Maybe

VERY ODD!

It can be hard for children to experience Christian fellowship and to become part of the worshipping community for many reasons including

● the strangeness of the building

● the odd clothing worn by some of those taking part

● the loneliness of being unaccompanied by a parent

● the insecurity of not knowing what to do next

● the inability to concentrate for long enough periods of time

● the long, unintelligible sentences, words and phrases that are used

● communication by words alone without any visual stimulus

● the lack of active learning with which they are comfortable

● the impatient expression on the faces of adults who do not understand

● their feeling of being patronized by some adults.

There is often a special service at the end of a holiday club or special event. It may follow the same theme and be appropriate for the children who have never been before, and they may enjoy it. But what will happen the following week? And the weeks after that?

GROWING APPROPRIATE

You may have to conclude that integrating new children into existing worship services just is not possible. The services are unchangeable. The congregation is resisting. The children themselves are not available at the right time.

If this is so, discuss with your vicar or church leader the possibility of 'growing' an appropriate service on a different day and possibly on premises that are familiar to the children. Encourage sympathetic church members, as well as the outreach leaders, to help establish this informal 'church plant' so that the children can be nurtured into and in faith.

ALL TOGETHER NOW!

Those who take the decision for your church to be a missionary church to children (that is, to reach out to the unchurched) should make sure that

● the whole congregation is involved in the plan and owns it

● those who cannot be involved with the outreach activities realize the importance of being fully committed to supporting and praying for those who can

● everyone is kept informed about up-to-the-minute prayer needs

● they create a prayer support structure in which people cannot avoid being involved.

Arrange **prayer support groups** to pray for the outreach, or ask existing home groups to pray for a specific event or group of leaders. You could also arrange special prayer groups during the outreach event itself.

Organize a **rota of individual pray-ers** during the time when the event is taking place. If it is a holiday club, for instance, make a week-long rota with the hours of the day marked on it. Encourage the congregation to pledge prayer for a specific hour or two so that the leaders involved in the outreach will know that someone is praying for them.

Request **intercessions during services** that will keep this missionary opportunity right at the top of the church's agenda.

Invite people to become **prayer parents**, especially those who would not naturally think they had a part to play in ministry among children. They could pray regularly for one contacted child by name. As a result, they might begin to have a more positive attitude towards the children who will eventually come into the church and to the changes that may have to be made to accommodate them.

SOWING AND GROWING

People who are involved in outreach to unchurched children often describe what they are doing as 'sowing seed'. They refer, of course, to the 'seed' of God's word which they long to plant in children's lives. But what will happen to the 'seed'? What signs of life and growth can we expect to see?

SOWING SEED

 On your own or in a group, find Matthew 13:1-9, 18-23 – the Parable of the Sower, and Jesus' explanation of it.

● Prepare four sheets of paper each with a simple outline of a child (or just a face) on it, and each with one of the following labels on it – 'path', 'rocks', 'thorns', 'good soil'.

● If there are four or more of you, share out the sheets. Ask each individual or small group to focus on their key word as you read the Bible verses out loud. Linked to this key word, they should write down on their sheet any thoughts they have about 'sowing' God's word in the lives of unchurched children.

● Discuss the following questions. Ask the individuals or small groups with the different sheets to note down any comments they hear that are appropriate to their key word:

■ How shall we scatter the 'seed' at our outreach event(s)?

■ How might it be received?

■ How shall we recognize where the 'seed' has landed?

■ What chance will the 'seed' have to grow?

■ What will 'birds', 'sun' and 'thorns' represent where the children live?

■ Are there ways in which we can prepare the 'soil' so that the 'seed' stands a better chance of growing?

● Finally, get the feedback from each sheet and use it to fuel your prayers.

● Decide what you can do to help the 'seed' to yield a good 'crop', though in the end, of course, only God can make the growth happen.

PREPARING THE SOIL

If you reach out to children who have no understanding of the Christian story and for whom the words 'God', 'Jesus' and 'Christ' are only expletives, you will need to prepare them carefully for the 'seed' of God's word.

Concentrate initially on befriending children, on building up their trust, and on showing them you care. Gradually they will discover that Christians have not landed from another planet, but are 'OK really'!

Do not judge about any aspect of a child's life-style, for example their language. The Holy Spirit will challenge them in time, if necessary. If their behaviour becomes unacceptable, however, do let them know that it is their behaviour you do not like, not *them*.

Rely on the Holy Spirit to help a child decide to become part of God's family. It must not be because you have pressurized them or, as they begin to 'own' the faith, because they are following the crowd. Spell out the cost of a changed life-style, of being misunderstood, of alienating old friends and of being the target of teasing. If they are still eager to respond to God, you can be sure that it really is the work of the Spirit. Then the sun can get on with trying to scorch! ■

'I DON'T SEE THE PROBLEM!'

I once explored the Parable of the Sower with a group of children's leaders. Coming from well-populated areas but leading small, struggling groups, most concentrated on the difficulties.

Into this despondency spoke an older voice: 'I don't see the problem. I'm a farmer. I prepare the soil, I plant the seed, I make sure it is watered regularly, I tend the young plants, and in the course of time, the crops are reaped. I approach my work with children in the same way.'

I discovered that Martin led the largest group represented by those leaders and that he came from the smallest village! Last year I visited a summer camp, and there was Martin, now drawing his pension, but still tending young plants!

SIGNS OF LIFE

So what signs of life shall we look for in the children we reach?

● Cut some leaf shapes from green paper and invite your team members to take a pile each.

● Get them to write on the leaves any changes in the lives of children which will show that God is beginning to work in them.

● Place a plant pot in the middle of the group and ask everyone to put their leaves into it.

● Bring out the leaves one by one, read them out and paste them on a large sheet of sky-blue paper in the shape of a tree.

Hopefully we shall discover that we are not looking just for the one major sign of a child making a 'commitment to Christ'. We might wait a long time for that and miss the encouragement of seeing the smaller but still significant things that God is doing in their lives. For instance, they may

■ be eager to come

■ be keen to listen to a Bible story

■ be ready to co-operate with leaders

■ want to ask questions

■ remember to bring something that has been requested

■ stop being defiant

■ no longer disrupt things

■ be generally more obedient

■ be no longer destructive

■ concentrate for longer periods of time

■ offer to take part or help

■ curb offensive language.

All these are signs that God is at work in them. Eventually there will be flowers as well as leaves as they

■ suggest topics for prayer

■ say a one-sentence prayer

■ see the needs of others

■ care for others

■ are concerned for others to hear about God

■ want to have a Bible and get stuck into it

■ display the fruit of the Spirit and minister the gifts of the Spirit.

How rewarding to be a missionary farmer for Jesus!

TIME FOR CHILDREN? YES!

We cannot watch seed grow, but in years to come, if we are patient, we may enjoy fruit from the tree!

The family of Pete and Dave only came to church on special occasions. The two boys heard about Jesus in their church primary school. They attended the school's lunchtime Good News Club, then started to come in early before school to read the Bible and pray together with a small group.

They went on a Pathfinder camp, and at different times made their own commitment to Christ. Back home they joined a nurture group. Eventually they became leaders on similar camps. Now, in their early twenties, Dave is a Christian teacher and Pete has been involved in bringing tough teenagers from a deprived city area in the North of England to know Jesus and to study the Bible.

I couldn't do that, but God enabled me to have a small part in bringing Pete and Dave to faith in him. Paul wrote in 1 Corinthians 3: 5-6, 'I planted the seed, Apollos watered it, but God made it grow.'

MORE TOOLS

CPAS Code	Title	Author and publisher
	HOW-TO RESOURCES	
92415	Caring for Children in Crèches and Toddler Groups	Ann Croft, CPAS 1995
03507	Children and Evangelism	Penny Frank, MarshallPickering 1992
	Groups without Frontiers	Terry Clutterham, Penny Frank, Phil Moon, CPAS 1996
82006	Reaching Young Families	Judith Wigley, CPAS
03576	Seen and Heard	Jackie Cray, Monarch 1995
03584	Sharing Jesus with Under-Fives	Janet Gaukroger, Crossway 1994
03484	Under-Fives and Their Families	Judith Wigley, MarshallPickering 1990
	All God's Children? Children's Evangelism in Crisis	National Society/Church House Publishing 1991
	Building New Bridges: Reaching and Teaching Children Through Mid-Week Clubs	Claire Gibb, National Society/ Church House Publishing 1996
	Children in The Way	National Society/Church House Publishing 1988
	Nuts and Bolts: The Scripture Union Guide to Running Holiday Clubs, Term-Time Missions and Other Special Events	Steve Hutchinson, Scripture Union 1996
	Reaching Children	Paul Butler, Scripture Union 1994
	Reaching Families	Paul Butler, Scripture Union 1995
	Under-Fives Welcome!	Kathleen Crawford, Scripture Union 1990
	PRACTICAL IDEAS	
03557	Praise, Play and Paint!	Jan Godfrey, National Society/ Church House Publishing 1995
03585	100 Instant Children's Talks	Sue Relf, Kingsway 1994
	Bounce! Exciting Resources for Use With 5-7s	Kathryn Copsey, Claire Derry, Scripture Union 1994
	Bright Ideas books	Scholastic
	Help! I'm a Parent!	CPAS 1995
	Here's One I Made Earlier	Kathryn Copsey, Scripture Union 1995
	Springboard: Helping 7-11 Year Olds Into the Bible	Sue Clutterham, Denise Trotter, Scripture Union 1989
	The Simply Wonderful Craftbook	Lois Rock, Lion
	COLLECTIVE WORSHIP AND SCHOOLS	
25120	Assembly Line	Andrew Smith, CPAS 1993
	Assemblies for Primary Schools	Margaret Cooling, RMEP
	Support Your Local School: A Guide to Opportunities for Church Involvement in Schools	Alison Farnell, Grahame Knox, Dennis Pethers, Andrew Smith, Schools Ministry Network 1996
	The Key to a Good Assembly	Claire Derry, Joanna Pitkin, Scripture Union
	52 Ideas for Junior Classroom Assemblies	Chris Chesterton, Pat Gutteridge, Monarch 1995
	DRAMA	
03617	Acting Up	Dave Hopwood, National Society/Church House Publishing 1995
25121	Much Ado About Something	Andrew Smith, CPAS 1994
	Much Ado About Something Else	Andrew Smith, CPAS 1996
	COUNSELLING MATERIALS	
	God's Children	Edited by Rachel Heathfield, CPAS 1996

HOLIDAY CLUB RESOURCES

Bodybuilders	Peter Graystone, Scripture Union 1993
The Light Factory	Janet Morgan, Angela Flynn, Scripture Union 1992
Newshounds	Peter Graystone, Scripture Union 1995
Secret Agents	Ron Fountain, Scripture Union 1987
Chattabox	Kathryn Copsey, Andy Saunders, Scripture Union 1996

The resources with a CPAS code are available from CPAS Sales on (01926) 334242 during the day, or on (01926) 335855 at any other time.

USEFUL ADDRESSES

(Sketch scripts and drama workshops for children)
Dave Hopwood, 106 Bitterne Drive, Woking, Surrey GU21 3JU

(Publicity and tracts)
Christian Publicity Organization, Garcia Estate, Canterbury Road, Worthing BN13 1BW
Tel: (01903) 264556

(Christian holiday activities for children)
CYFA Pathfinder Ventures Ltd, Athena Drive, Tachbrook Park, Warwick CV34 6NG
Tel: (01926) 334242

Crusaders, 2 Romeland Hill, St Albans AL3 4ET
Tel: (01727) 855422

Covenanters, 11/13 Lower Hillgate, Stockport, Cheshire SK1 1JQ
Tel: (0161) 474 1262

Scripture Union Holiday Activities, 207 Queensway, Bletchley, Milton Keynes MK2 2EB
Tel: (01908) 856000

(Advice on running residentials with children)
Christian Camping International, PO Box 169, Coventry CV1 4PW
Tel: (01203) 559099

(Collective worship and other Christian work in schools)
Scripture Union in Schools, 207 Queensway, Bletchley, Milton Keynes, MK2 2EB
Tel: (01908) 856000

Stapleford RE Resources Project, Stapleford House Education Centre, Wesley Place, Stapleford, Nottingham NG9 8DP
Tel: (0115) 939 6270

The Malachi Community Trust, 619 Bordesley Green, Bordesley, Birmingham B9 5XZ